LA

CF 0450 XC

SPIT
a LIFE in BATTLES

FEATURING ILLUSTRATIONS BY

Sam Rodriguez

Michelle Kwon

Turtleboat

Aaron Kai

Brian Yoon

SPIT

a LIFE in BATTLES

JONNIE PARK
AKA DUMBFOUNDEAD

WITH DONNIE KWAK

FOREWORD BY ANDERSON .PAAK

THIRD STATE BOOKS

SAN FRANCISCO

SPIT: A LIFE IN BATTLES
by Jonnie Park with Donnie Kwak

Published by Third State Books
93 Cumberland Street
San Francisco, CA 94110
Visit us at www.thirdstatebooks.com

Edited by Charles Kim and Stephanie Lim
First edition: April 2026
ISBN 979-8-89013-039-6 (hardcover)
979-8-89013-041-9 (e-book)
979-8-89013-042-6 (audiobook)

Cover design by Brian Hung
Text design by Kathryn E. Campbell
Front endpaper illustration: "Persimmons and Pan Dulce" by Sam Rodriguez
"Murals" photo: Alex Oh
Cover image and Park author photo: Lenne Chai
Kwak author photo: Stephen Han

To the women who made me battle-ready

I ain't a killer, but don't push me

—2Pac

CONTENTS

FOREWORD

Anderson .Paak

I knew the legend of Dumbfoundead before I ever met him.

I'd just moved to Los Angeles, a hungry musician trying to support a wife and a newborn son. Everywhere I went, people told me the same thing: "You need to meet Dumb." I heard his name for weeks. *Who is this fool?* So, I looked him up and found a bunch of battle-rap videos from a world I knew nothing about. His clips were going viral, and I could see why. Dumb had a wholesome undertone that set him apart. Most battle rappers came off as vindictive, talking about dead grandmas or leaning into racist jokes. Dumb didn't need any of that. He was smart, witty, and charming. And of course, he was the lone Asian American kid in the middle of the hood, battling the best of the best, which made me want to root for him.

I was like, *Oh, he's dope.* But I was also thinking, *How am I gonna meet this dude? He's already huge.* As luck would have it, Dumb was already tracking me down through mutual friends. We first met backstage at one of my gigs. Within seconds, I knew we'd get along, and he made me feel comfortable off the bat. But what really impressed me was what came next, when he pulled me into his world.

I'm telling you: Dumb was the Michael Jackson of Ktown. At the time, I didn't personally know anyone more famous than him. He took my broke ass around and showed me a whole world of bars, clubs, and noraebangs I didn't know existed. I knew he was a real one the night we went to a secret afterhours spot, and they wouldn't let me in because I wasn't Korean enough. Dumb raised hell at the door: "If all of us can't get in, none of us are going in!" (We got in.) He had a way of making you let your guard down. And it wasn't just me. Everybody in Ktown knew Dumb and loved him. He was that guy.

On the music side, I quickly realized Dumb was ten steps ahead of me. I'd met plenty of rappers who talked about wanting to collaborate, but Dumb was the first to say, "Pull up, I've got a studio session booked." He already had a whole infrastructure in place. He introduced me to his DJ, his manager, his videographer. It tripped me out that he had a person who could film him, edit the video, and have it online the very next day. They were booking shows, doing meet-and-greets, selling thousands of T-shirts, doing all kinds of shit—and all of this without a label. I remember thinking, *This dude is doing it all by himself. He's not waiting on anybody.* And that mindset rubbed off on me. Dumb built a well-oiled machine without anyone giving him permission to do it.

Plus, Dumb believed in me. "I think you're gonna be the biggest thing," he told me. "I'll do anything I can to help." I worked on his *DFD* album, and then he asked me to produce the entire next one, *Take the Stares*—the first time anybody trusted me to do so. I became his Flavor Flav on the road, and he'd let me spit my own joints. That experience helped shape my artistry and gave me access to a fanbase that was way bigger than mine. Mind you, I was dead broke and felt like a burden most of the time. Dumb would let me use his car and borrow money, and even let my whole family live in his apartment while he was on tour. Whatever I needed—what was his was mine. I saw how hard he worked: freestyling for hours at parties, captivating the whole room, then waking up the next day and grinding. Work hard, play hard.

While I was watching him grow, I was putting in the hours to get ready for my turn. That's when I changed from Breezy Lovejoy to Anderson .Paak. Dumb gave me unlimited access to his studio, and I remember riding my bike for miles to use it when he wasn't there. It was during one of those solo sessions that I wrote and recorded a song called "Suede." It eventually made its way to Dr. Dre, and boom, the rest is history. Through it all, Dumb stayed solid. Sometimes, when things start popping, you don't get to keep the same circle. People treat you differently—even the ones you've known forever. It can get uncomfortable. You become more guarded. But Dumb never changed. Wherever I was in my career or personal life, he was there. Loyal, consistent. It was always important for me to keep that connection.

Our bond runs deep. Like me, Dumb grew up around trauma and learned to cope through humor and music. That's how both of us survived childhood. Now that we're grown, we don't have to live like that anymore, but we still got that dog in us. We both carry that chip on our shoulder. We love hearing someone tell us we can't do something. To this day, I'm still inspired by him, watching him evolve again and again. He walked away from battling to make albums, became an early YouTube creator, stepped back from music to do stand-up and write for TV, and now he's acting in and producing films. That evolution matters—not just to me, but to the culture he came up in. He's the reason I was able to direct my first movie,

K-POPS!, which he also co-produced and co-stars in. It felt like déjà vu, back to when we were just starting out. Dumb stays one step ahead of me, but we're always synced on where he's headed. The sky's the limit.

Now he's got a book, and rightfully so. Dumb opened a lot of doors, especially for Asian Americans in hip-hop. Most of them didn't have to go through what he did, and I don't know if they would've survived it. What I'm saying is: Dude is built different. But Dumb isn't just a pioneer for Asian Americans; he's a pioneer, period. He shouldn't only be talked about in the Asian American landscape. He's bigger than that. Yet there are pros and cons to being so early. Sometimes the people who do the most for the culture get overlooked because they were ahead of their time. The real appreciation comes later, if at all.

Luckily, you don't have to wait. You're about to read his memoir. I'm proud of my brother. He'll always have my respect for building a life without waiting to be chosen. I can't wait for you to get to know Dumb like I do. Yes Lawd!

INTRO

Spit. An ugly word. It conjures images of rage, like "spitting mad." As a noun, it's disgusting. As a verb, it's disrespectful. Spit in front of my dad? Ass whooping. Spit in Singapore? Jail time.

But it's beautiful too. Freeing. Growing up, I was told, "Shut up." At my first cypher, they said, "Spit something." That's why they say rappers spit. A defiant release of all we've been told to swallow, everything you're not supposed to say. It becomes a compulsion. A salivating urge, a gut instinct. It is disrespectful, but it can also earn you respect—and that's its power.

Spit reminds me of my father's anger and of a wild freestyle cypher. But most of all, it's a mano-a-mano rap battle, two faces so close that flecks hit each other like shrapnel. When they spit, you spit back.

A Life. I was born in Argentina, smuggled into America over the Mexican border when I was three, and raised in Koreatown, Los Angeles. A child of the 1992 riots. Those streets shaped me.

My gift of gab showed up as soon as I could talk, entertaining my mom and my sister, two years younger. I craved attention. Not easy to find in a household like mine. Immigrant parents, thankless jobs, long hours. Downtown stores peddling trinkets. Dad drinking, distant, violent. Mom coping, depressed. Left to my own devices, I broke rules before I learned them. Trial and error. Making shit up on the fly. Talking my way out of trouble. Classroom as stage. Wordplay made kids laugh. Fast tongue, freestyled for fun. Street smart, far from dumb. I needed adoration; the lunch table gave it. I wanted to feel special. Unique. I was "Chino." The only Asian kid in every crew I was in: The block boys in Ktown. The stoner kids at school. The rap scene I stumbled into. I gatekept the Chino role. I was representing my people without even knowing it.

Teenage years, home life was worse than ever. Constant battleground. My parents split. My life, forties and weed. An outcast, a pothead, a nerd, a weirdo, a loser. Bouncing between high schools, barely showing up. Roaming around Ktown without a plan. Dropped out in the tenth grade—my parents didn't even notice. Life in shambles. Hunting for a sanctuary, a way out. I found it at an open mic in South Central.

In Battles. Battle rap is spoken word. Debate. Wrestling. Theater. Stand-up. Except the heckler is on stage with equal time to roast you. Three rounds. Cleverness and confidence in equal measure. Insults become punchlines, weave into rhymes so intricate, so dense, so scathing that they can make a crowd explode. Its approval powers you forward. To win, you have to dish it—and take it too. Black, white, Latino, Asian. Big, small, young, old. You learn what rattles your opponent. You find what rattles you.

It started on the corner of 43rd and Leimert. Project Blowed, where the best rappers in the city tested their skills. Every Thursday night till the early morning. The cornerstone of my journey in hip-hop and in life. Freestyles, battles, performances. No rules, no boundaries. Not for the weak or the wack. I was a fifteen-year-old Peter Parker when I wandered in; the validation I got there was the spider bite. It turned Jonnie into Dumbfoundead. Cyphers overflowing with rappers who had something to prove. My superpower unleashed: quick improv, sharp wit, comedic timing. Soon after, thick skin, bulletproof confidence. Invisible at home, but front and center here. I just wanted to be seen. At Blowed, I met my mentors, friends, foes. The dysfunctional family adopted me, a scruffy Korean teenager looking for a home. I became one of them. Under pressure, I did more than survive. I thrived.

Project Blowed honed my skill in battle rap, and it became the foundation of my life. Only once I made it into a career did I realize it could be one. I charted my own path, accepted all challengers. Crowned a battle legend before I turned twenty-five. Recorded music, dropped albums, toured colleges—an unwitting icon to Asian Americans who needed one. Made Dumbfoundead a brand, a business. Traveled to Korea to reconnect with my roots. Flipped the script on Asian-male stereotypes. Weak, timid? No. Loud, unruly. The pride of Ktown, sometimes the disgrace. Won battles; lost some too. Still talked my way out of trouble—with girls, managers, gangstas. Prepared, yet never prepared. Freestyled through the rap life and real life. Locked in with kindred spirits: Anderson .Paak, Awkwafina, Jay Park, collaborators before *Billboard* and the billboards. Addictions formed, vices multiplied. Relationships deteriorated. The battles grew more serious. Some I couldn't freestyle my way out of. I was an expert at reading opponents. I was less good at reading myself.

Frame life as a battle, and you'll always be fighting something.

Opponents are everywhere, real and invisible. The competitive spirit rages, fueled by pettiness. Grudges, perceived slights. Fear of being underestimated, chip on my shoulder. Driven by hate, the desire to prove people wrong. The need for outside validation to determine a winner—if there ever really is one.

My parents fought their own battles. With each other, with unfamiliar lands, with bad businesses, with their kids. Life spit at them, and they took it, just to survive. They endured. I refused. That American audacity to just not give a fuck. To spit back.

Spit, in the end, can also be healing. Lick the wound and fight on. Face and conquer the battle within. Find love. Then you can win the war.

I once struggled to come up with enough material to fill a song. I now have enough to fill a book. This is *Spit: A Life in Battles.*

CHAPTER ONE

APPA

The Spoon Test. 1996, Koreatown, L.A.

Anyone who's had a meal with me knows that I eat *really* fast—like, mukbang, Kobayashi, prison-mess-hall fast. As if I were racing to clear my plate. What most people don't know is that this eating habit comes from survival instinct. I have my father to thank for that. Growing up, mealtime was never a moment to relax. It was a stressful operation to get in and out of before the tension boiled over.

As a kid, I developed something I called the "spoon test," which I applied to my dad when we ate as a family. Mind you, this wasn't every night, but only on the occasions when he actually made it home for dinner, instead of carousing with his buddies over endless bottles of soju.

I'll break it down and set the scene for you:

It's a cloudy fall evening. Inside our Koreatown apartment, my mother is cooking up her usual dishes, a mishmash of Korean, American, and Latin American: kimchi jjigae with Spam, kkaennip ssam, omurice, and milanesa, a breaded meat dish popular in Argentina. A few blocks away on Western Avenue is California Market, my mom's go-to for groceries—the same spot where the "rooftop Koreans" were famously photographed protecting their stores with rifles during the 1992 riots. Four years have passed since then, but the air in Koreatown still feels charged.

While my mom is cooking, my eight-year-old sister Natalia and I are mindlessly watching *The Fresh Prince of Bel-Air* or any number of syndicated sitcoms featuring a happy American household: *Family Matters, Full House, Step by Step.* With the smell of Korean comfort food wafting through the apartment, we, too, might seem like a portrait of domestic tranquility. But in reality, we're all anxiously awaiting my father's arrival from his shop in downtown L.A.

The dread sets in the second I hear his keys jingling in the doorway. Once he walks in, my stomach tightens, and I feel a prickle beneath my skin. His presence sucks all the air out of the room. There's no "How was school today, kids?" when my dad comes home. He doesn't want to talk to anyone—not my mom, my sister, or me. He wants to be left alone. No banter, no silly stuff. He wants silence so he can smoke a Marlboro Light and lie on the black leather couch with a Korean newspaper until dinner is ready. He doesn't give a shit about secondhand smoke, and we don't know better at that age. The tension propels me into my room. My mom continues to cook, while Natalia, quiet and obedient, sets the table.

Soon, dinner is served, rice bowls and a sprawl of banchan spread out before us. The mood is uneasy but relatively calm. In the quiet, it's uncertain whether he's mad about something. We just sit in fear of an eruption. Everything seems fine—until it's not.

Now seated at the dinner table, my dad dips his spoon into the jjigae, but he is focusing on me. I know something is about to trigger him; I'm just not sure what. An anxiety-inducing game show plays in my head: *What Will Piss Dad Off Today?* He lifts the spoon to his mouth. Then he stops.

The image terrifies me: My father holds a spoonful of broth suspended in midair for what feels like an eternity. I watch the spoon carefully, similar to how the camera zooms in on that glass of water in *Jurassic Park*. His gaze locks on me. I flush from the heat of his narrowing eyes. The pace of my chewing quickens.

Now, the spoon test. If it continues its path into his mouth and he finishes that bite, we're good. I can breathe again, scarf down the rest of my plate, excuse myself from the table, and escape back to my room. But if the spoon never makes it to his mouth? Well, then it's on. He's going to slam it back into the soup bowl, and all hell will break loose.

Today, the spoon doesn't make it. Dad's voice shatters the silence. He bubbles over with complaints, as if he'd been mentally building a list since he arrived home. The gripes stream out of his mouth along with tiny flecks of food.

"Fix your posture!" he barks at me.

I'm ten years old! Who cares about posture when they're ten? While I don't dare speak the words out loud, my mind spits comebacks as I chew silently.

"What's wrong with your hair?"

Look at your goofy-ass hair, Dad. You're gonna complain about mine?

"Why are you wearing that chain, you want to be Black?"

Well . . . maybe, yes?

Next, he fixates on my size, or lack thereof. He was obsessed that I wasn't growing at the same rate as my peers. My XXXL Mecca shirt and Phat Farm pants, both scored from Ross Dress for Less (aka Broke Boy Heaven), make me look comically small. He takes his spoon, shovels rice onto it from his bowl, and shoves it toward my face, growling, "Eat, you little brat." It's never "Eat well, son, so you can grow up healthy." Instead, it's "What's wrong with you? Why are you so small?" I sit there crying while eating, getting scolded for something I have no control over.

My dad pauses for a moment and sighs, exhausted by his diatribe. I'm scared and stuttering, trying to divert his anger somehow and not escalate the situation.

My mom is on the side, pleading, "Leave him alone."

My dad starts yelling at her. His verbal abuse can easily escalate to physical violence, directed at my mom or me. Or both. But this time, he hurls his spoon at the wall. Kimchi-stew juice splatters against the white surface like blood. I'm paralyzed by fear, bracing myself for Dad to raise his now empty hand against my mother or me. Maybe he's tired, or just over it, but he suddenly stands, fishes out another spoon from a drawer, and sits back down to continue eating as if nothing happened. I race to finish another bite or two and get the fuck away from the dinner table.

And scene.

That's why I eat so fast as an adult. Like I said: survival instinct.

The spoon test went badly more times than I can count. In fact, I spent most of my childhood avoiding interaction altogether with my father, who was a selfish, negligent, raging alcoholic. After my parents split when I was thirteen, I felt nothing but relief. I've repressed a lot of childhood memories, but some simply never existed at all: my parents kissing, holding hands, or sharing a single happy moment between them. I don't remember my father ever complimenting me—well, maybe once, when I finally cut the hair he detested. "You see, now you look like a real man!"

My parents were born in Korea, met in Argentina, and chased the American dream in downtown Los Angeles. But that dream, elusive as it was, destroyed our family. Relentless work unlocked nothing but more relentless work, barely keeping us afloat. No savvy investments or careful saving ever turned our fortunes around. Instead of moving to a nice house in the suburbs, we shuffled from one cramped Koreatown apartment to another. The constant struggle deepened my dad's bitterness and drove him away from us, leaving my mom depressed and shut down.

As I started pursuing my own career in entertainment, a large part of what fueled me was a need to finish the job my parents couldn't—whatever that "job" was supposed to be. I wasn't trying to carry the torch so much as trying to reignite whatever weak flame remained. Still, I have to thank my dad for creating such a hostile home environment, because it forced me to flee the house and find a new family. I also must thank my mom—as well as the human smugglers who snuck her, my sister, and me over the Mexican border in 1989—for getting me to the States in the first place. Long before we feared my dad's anger, we feared the heat, the coyotes, and the endless desert.

Coyotes. 1989, Mexico–Texas Border

My family was living in Argentina, in a town called Solano, about fifteen miles south of Buenos Aires. When I was two, my father got the itch and sought greener pastures in America. Instead of securing a visa, he entered the country as a tourist and headed for Los Angeles, where his friends helped him find work off the books. Over a year later, he was ready for his wife and two kids to join him, but he didn't have the right paperwork to bring us over legally. In the late 1980s, unless you had connections, sponsors in America, or some special skill, the US wasn't exactly doling out visas for families like ours. Instead, my dad sent money for us to fly from Buenos Aires to Mexico City, where he had arranged for "coyotes"—paid human smugglers—to slip us through the US border.

Maybe my dad already knew how risky this expedition would be, but I don't think my mother had any idea of the hardship to come. We embarked on a dangerous journey from Mexico City to the border that took over eleven days in blazing heat, walking and riding in the backs of trucks. I have only the faintest of memories of that trek, mere glimpses and fuzzy images; my mother, on the other hand, recalls it all with painful clarity. Picture a tiny Korean woman with an infant daughter, Natalia, strapped to her back and a toddler son clutching her hand, among a dozen or so people desperate to enter the land of opportunity. There were migrants from Colombia and Chile and even other Asian families, who were the unfriendliest of the group. Two Korean men who started the trip with us somehow flagged down a ride in the middle of the voyage and abandoned the rest of us. We were traveling together, but it was every family for itself.

Meanwhile, the coyotes were not a comforting bunch: bearded, gruff Mexican men who carried guns and knives and herded us like sheep. When we stopped at night to sleep, usually in an empty house in some eerie, isolated village, they drank alcohol and did drugs, occasionally shining flashlights at us in a taunting manner. Early in the trek, one of the coyotes eyed my mother from head to toe with a lewd smirk. For the remainder of the trip, my mom didn't wash her face or brush her teeth. She wore long, loose clothes and let her hair grow wild. Terrified that these men might target her in a vulnerable moment, she made her appearance as rough as possible.

On an unbearably hot day, the coyotes promised the group that they'd bring back food and water if we gave them some money. Instead, they left us in the desert and didn't return until many hours later. My mom told me later that she couldn't stop crying, thinking that we'd never make it to America, as Natalia pleaded desperately, "Agua, agua." To lighten the mood and cheer my sister up, I started packing sand and dirt, fashioning it into a "cake." According to my mother, I started singing "Happy Birthday" in Korean, pretending to cut it and feed it to her. My mom said I was remarkably calm despite everything going on. I guess you could call that my first performance—and it was a hit. Call me Toddler of the Year.

The initial discomfort of the first few days gave way to a monotonous toil. As we got closer to the border, our fear subsided, replaced by a quiet determination to reach our final destination. After we had finally crossed the border into Texas—my mother recalls the entry being surprisingly smooth and uneventful—we flew to L.A. to begin our new life.

I can't imagine what the experience must've been like for my mother, trying to keep two babies quiet, not knowing if we'd make it to the other side. Even though I was too young to remember it fully, it's something I'll never forget.

And, on that note, fuck ICE.

Seoul to Solano. 1970s–1980s, Paraguay and Argentina

You're probably wondering how a Korean family got to Argentina in the first place. Like many details about my parents' lives, their origin story has only been explained to me in bits and pieces.

My mother grew up in Seoul with her parents and two brothers; the younger sibling, who was intellectually disabled, had a beautiful singing voice and could play guitar. Her mother ran a small market stall near a church, while her father worked alongside an American missionary at a place called Shalom House, about twenty-five miles north of the capital. My grandparents were humble, simple people, devout churchgoers who were strict but kind. Mom doesn't ever recall seeing them fight, not even once.

When my mom was sixteen, her family moved to Paraguay, one of the thousands of Korean families who immigrated to South America in the 1960s and '70s, when postwar South Korea was still a poor, struggling country. They lived in Paraguay for seven years, selling clothes door to door and assimilating into South American culture. Outside of work, they learned Spanish and drank maté in communal circles with their neighbors. At school, my mom's classmates nicknamed her Kitty because they thought she looked like a kitty doll that was popular in the 1970s. The nickname stuck with her the rest of her life.

At twenty-three, my mother and her family moved just outside of Buenos Aires, Argentina, the country with the second-largest Korean population in South America (after Brazil). By the mid-1980s, it had roughly fifty thousand Korean residents, and many of them worked in the garment industry. My mom, always bright and cheerful, lived a simple and carefree life there, but as her brother's mental-health challenges worsened, she spent a lot of time taking care of him while her parents worked.

Meanwhile, my dad arrived straight from Seoul to Argentina in his twenties. He had allegedly caused some trouble running around with different women in Korea, so his father brought him to South America, intending to force him to settle down and possibly marry. Dad renamed himself Pablo and made some business connections in the capital city. He met Kitty through mutual friends at a party and fell for her. She remembers him as good-looking and confident, perhaps a bit shameless, with the attitude of a boss even though he was aimless and unemployed. I suppose it was his bold personality—or his parents' desire for him to find a wife—that compelled him to propose to her after only three dates.

"I'll marry you," he said matter-of-factly, grinning like it was a done deal.

My mom, eager to leave the family home and the responsibility of looking after her sibling, replied simply, "Why not?" How romantic.

Right after they married, my parents opened a clothing store in Solano, and it was very successful. However, it wasn't long until my mom started to realize that my dad wasn't the most dependable spouse. In fact, he was kind of an asshole. During the daily siestas that shuttered the local shops for a few hours, my dad would venture into downtown Buenos Aires, ostensibly to buy supplies, but often lingering to drink with friends, leaving my mom to manage the store.

She wondered how he could disappear for so long while she toiled in the shop alone.

It was no different the day I was born, February 18, 1986. My pregnant mom worked through the morning, came home for lunch, and told my grandmother, "I think the baby is coming soon. I'll walk to the hospital. Can you mind the store?" She trudged all the way to the hospital by herself, and after some excruciating hours, gave birth to me. "Out of nowhere, you just came out," she'd tell me later.

And my dad? He never showed up. He was in Buenos Aires all day and only arrived back home late at night. It was the exact same scenario when Natalia was born two years later: My mom gave birth at the hospital alone, and my dad was MIA for hours afterward.

My mom returned to work just days after each of her kids was born; my dad, it seems, was already plotting his next chapter.

Something Special. Late 1980s–1990s, Koreatown, L.A.

When I close my eyes and conjure an image of my dad, I can't quite picture his face. Instead, I see his silhouette on the couch, his head obscured behind a newspaper, cigarette smoke curling up to the ceiling. In the background, there's a big TV airing a golf match. For most of my childhood, it was as if he weren't even there. He was hiding from everything: us, his failures, and himself.

To be fair, American life wasn't easy for him. Shortly after my sister was born, in spring 1988, he left Argentina to find work in downtown L.A. There, Koreans were starting to build what became known as the "jobber" (or jaba in Konglish) market, a network of Korean immigrant wholesalers who would soon take over L.A.'s fashion district. These family-run businesses sold clothing, accessories, and other products wholesale to retailers. The jaba market was fiercely competitive, with long hours and Industrial Revolution–style working conditions. For Korean American (KA) immigrants, it was a route to claw their way into the American economy, relying on their resourcefulness and tenacity to get ahead—some getting much further than others. Korean families in L.A. were divided into the haves and have-nots, and we were firmly among the latter.

Probably the biggest success story to come out of the jaba market was the Chang family, whom I got to know through our Korean church. My parents weren't even that religious, but because every good Korean goes to church on Sundays, so, too, did we. It was called the Great Vision Church, on Normandie and 5th, in the heart of Koreatown. Like most Korean churches in America, it was also home to weekend Korean school, where young Korean Americans like myself begrudgingly took language classes and taekwondo.

The Changs had two daughters, Linda and Esther. The latter was close to my age, and one time, I called her uglier than a Garbage Pail Kid (maybe my first roast?), though honestly, I had a secret crush on her. She burst into tears. Well, Linda and Esther got the last laugh, because their parents, who started from the ground up like mine did, revolutionized "fast fashion" as a retail concept and turned it into the Forever 21 empire. Rather than making fun of Esther, I should've been planting seeds to one day marry into her clan.

My dad worked for a Korean family at a jewelry store called Something Special, in Santee Alley, the Canal Street of L.A., where a lot of bootleg products were sold. He was barely ever home in those days, waking up at 5:30 a.m. to commute the five or so miles to downtown L.A. Just like in Argentina, he played as much as he worked. On most nights or on days off, he'd go out drinking at bars and karaoke parlors. Otherwise, he played golf. Yes, even the brokest Korean dad can find a way to support his addiction to the game.

Although my mom was busy working at the shop and raising Natalia and me, she also had her own random side hustles. At barely five years old, I would sit beside her in the sweatshop-like basement of an apartment, helping her drop ink cartridges into ballpoint pen shells and putting them in boxes. She says I was a sweet and adorable child, a magnet for affection from older aunties. What can I say? I've always known how to work a crowd.

In fact, when she wasn't weighed down by her crushing responsibilities, my mom was a playful, funny character in her own right. We grew up watching *I Love Lucy* reruns because my mom was such a huge fan. Reenacting scenes from the show came naturally to her, with all the animated energy of Lucille Ball, even in Korean. I think part of my desire to perform comes from that side of her. If my dad had allowed her to express herself more, she likely wouldn't have become so withdrawn and quiet throughout my childhood. In hindsight, it's ironic to compare my mom to Lucy, because in real life, Lucille Ball and her husband, Desi Arnaz, also had domestic disputes over his infidelity and alcohol abuse. Now I know how Little Ricky must have felt. It seemed like my dad was in another world, and most of the time, he was. I sympathize with him to a certain extent, because he was grinding under the eye of a more prosperous Korean family. Eventually, he was named manager at Something Special, but he couldn't seem to get over the hump, no matter how hard he tried. And speaking of hump, he was also having a secret affair with the last person he should've been creeping with.

The Boss's Wife. Mid-1990s, Hancock Park, L.A.

When I was eight, my dad convinced my mom to take Natalia and me on a weekend outing to Santa Barbara, a two-hour drive from L.A., while he stayed behind. My Spidey senses could already tell something was wrong between them. Looking back, I realize that my mom must've known deep down he was cheating on her, but couldn't yet confront him. She needed hard proof.

All I remember from that trip was my mom fretting, calling home continually from a pay phone, paranoid about my dad's whereabouts. When she wasn't trying to reach him, she murmured to herself about another woman, who I later found out was the boss's wife. I dissociated in those moments—I could hear her, but I couldn't really *hear* her. I just observed how my mom was clearly acting beside herself and distant from Natalia and me. I felt helpless and angry at my dad's manipulation. He'd made the trip seem like a gift, but it was really to get us out of his way. Sadly, it's one of the few childhood trips I remember.

What made things worse was that our family had become friends with my dad's boss's family. The first time I realized we were truly poor was when we visited their house. They lived in Hancock Park, only a couple of miles from Koreatown, but a world away—like the Gangnam to our Pyongyang—where many celebrities lived. I always thought of Hancock Park as the best place to go on Halloween. Koreatown residents would drop seaweed packs in your bucket, while Hancock folks gave you full-size Twix and Warheads. When I saw the inside of the boss's house, it blew my mind. It was insanely big—not cramped and cluttered like our place—with rooms to spare. The boss and his wife had two sons and a daughter; their eldest son was my age, and their daughter was the same age as Natalia. We got to know the kids pretty well. Because we were relatively new to the country and scraping by financially, the boss's family looked out for us and invited us over regularly. Plus, the kids had a Super Nintendo, and that alone made me like them.

Still, hanging out with the boss's family marked the beginning of my resentment toward my own parents about their inability to create this lifestyle for us. When Koreatown families became successful, they usually moved to Hancock Park or farther out to suburbs like Glendale or La Crescenta. We never left; my parents never bought property, and I'd lived in Ktown apartments my whole life. My dad compared us to other families a lot. Why couldn't we be industrious and well-behaved like the kids of other people he knew in the jaba market? He seemed to adore those kids while harboring some special hatred for his own family, as if it were somehow our fault that he couldn't save money and get us out of Ktown.

It was definitely his fault that we stopped being friends with his boss's family, though. One day, my mom finally got the receipts she needed to prove her case. That morning, in a torrential downpour, my dad left home early to "play golf." When he came back that night, instead of bringing food home for the whole family like other dads might, he brought enough dinner for himself and ate it at the dining table. Classic dad. As he did so, my mom acted on a premonition and went outside to check his car. It was there, underneath the floor mat, that she found a love letter written by the boss's wife.

"When I see you walking away, my heart aches," it read.

The next scene played out like a K-drama: My mom went back upstairs to the apartment and poured herself a huge glass of whiskey.

Though she was never a heavy drinker, she chugged it straight. Her face turned beet red from Asian glow. My dad sat at the dinner table, unaware of what she had just discovered.

She approached him, her voice steady. "You've put me through so much. I don't need anything from you. Let's divorce."

He snickered. "If you want to separate, I'll agree," he said. "But only if I see you dead first."

Without hesitation, she grabbed a knife from the kitchen and handed it to him. "Kill me, then. Go ahead and kill me," she replied, as calmly as if she were requesting a back rub.

Maybe it was her words or the unflinching tone in which she delivered them, but my dad got spooked, the knife heavy in his hand. "You're crazy," he muttered shakily, then bolted to the bathroom and locked the door. Turns out he wasn't so tough when confronted.

Not yet satisfied, my mom chose to confront my dad's mistress the following week. In the past, she had pretended to be a trusted confidante, someone my mom could talk to when things weren't going well at home. This time, my mom called her with other intentions.

"Can I stop by your house?"

Suspicious, the boss's wife panicked and suggested meeting at a local café instead. As my mom left, my dad snuck out to follow her to her destination.

According to my mother, another dramatic scene ensued. Seated across from my dad and his mistress, she handed over the love letter and told the boss's wife to read it. Before presenting it to her, my mom had made a copy and left it with a friend in the neighborhood, fearful of what an angered rich lady might do impulsively.

However, the boss's wife played dumb.

"What's going on?" she asked, insisting it was all a misunderstanding.

My dad started cursing and calling my mom crazy.

Undeterred, my mom lit into them both, yelling at my dad, "If you didn't want to be with me, you could've just divorced me. Instead, you've humiliated me."

Embarrassed by the scolding, my dad slunk out of the café. His mistress tried to make nice with my mom, suggesting that she could pay her way through cosmetology school, since my mom had expressed an interest in becoming a beautician. My mom, shocked at the woman's shamelessness, refused and walked out. When she returned home, she found my dad pacing around in his underwear. In a rare moment of weakness, he desperately apologized, practically begging for forgiveness.

"I'm only doing this for the kids," she told him.

And so, my mom and dad stayed together despite the affair. She accepted it and moved on. I suppose the boss's wife did too, because my dad didn't stop working at Something Special for a few more years. However, from that moment forward, we never hung out with the boss's kids again. No more Super Nintendo for us. Game over.

"Gangsta's Paradise." 1995, Downtown L.A.

When my dad stopped working at Something Special, my parents opened two downtown shops of their own. They worked at both stores interchangeably. First, there was Kitty Jewelry, named after my mother, which sold more cheap accessories than fine jewelry. Around the corner, a block away from both the Toy District and Skid Row, he opened Pax Trading, a play on Park, our family name. Pax Trading sold all kinds of knickknacks, from scrunchies to little toys and trinkets. Since I was around the store a lot, I was on top of nineties toy trends—laser pointers, Razor scooters, and the like—because we stocked bootleg versions of them. We sold pink Teletubbies and a Spice Girls doll called Spooky Spice, who spoke with a Spanish accent—the equivalent to what Lafufus are today.

Pax was a stand-alone store, but Kitty was more like a storefront in a swap-meet type of market, where all kinds of goods were peddled under one roof. It was a sprawling, mazelike space, with vendor stalls separated by metal gates that were pulled shut at closing time. Since there were no walls, I'd run around the whole swap meet, playing hide-and-seek with other downtown Latino and Korean kids. I credit that place for putting me on the path to a rap career. My parents couldn't afford a babysitter, so they brought Natalia and me to work all the time when we were in elementary school. We spent our spring and summer breaks hanging around the two stores.

Right next to Kitty Jewelry was an electronics store owned by an Indian dude. It sold all the hood party accessories: smoke machines, sirens, and lighting systems. Total sensory overload. But those weren't the hottest items for sale. Since this was the nineties, the main attractions were the boomboxes lined up near the register. And if you wanted to purchase one, you weren't trying to hear the Smashing Pumpkins. All the sound systems were tuned to either of L.A.'s two main hip-hop stations, Power 106 and 92.3 The Beat, at ear-splitting volumes. Every day my impressionable young ears were soaking in West Coast rap from Snoop Doggy Dogg, Ice Cube, and the one song that seemed to rule the entire year: "Gangsta's Paradise" by Coolio, from the *Dangerous Minds* film soundtrack. Hip-hop invaded my brain and never left. I became fascinated with the way rappers strung their words together, painting vivid pictures of life around them in rhyme. I started to mimic their styles and began writing some verses of my own.

The chaos wasn't limited to the electronics store next door. All the downtown shops were overstimulating. Every inch of space was filled with some kind of product—shelves upon shelves of endless plastic and polyester. (Maybe it explains why my attention span is so short.) I grew up in this intense, uneasy postriot environment, surrounded by Latinos, Korean American shop owners, and a lot of unhoused people. The shop owners had sons and daughters who were running amok downtown like me. We'd all meet up and rove around in packs, shoplifting trinkets and comparing our hauls.

Of course, I also had to lend a hand at Pax, which was like every store in the area. Worthless items were stacked from the ground up, in all sorts of colors and shapes. The main sound I heard everywhere was the zip of packing tape being used by my dad or a Mexican employee or me to seal cardboard boxes. It's the holy trinity of the wholesale market: dollies, boxes, and tape dispensers. The stores sold goods to one another. I'd often hear my dad negotiating in Spanish—"Mi amigo, por favor"—or another Latino dude haggling with him. They'd both be muttering "That's cheap" or "This is good quality" in their respective languages as they surveyed the goods and bought whatever they needed in bulk.

Having spent so much time in South America, my mom and dad were fluent in Spanish. And because they never made any American friends and only dealt with Koreans or the Latinos they did business with, they still speak barely any English, even to this day. In L.A., you can apparently get around for over thirty years without learning English if you have those two other languages down pat.

Despite it being a fairly successful enterprise, Kitty Jewelry shuttered a few years after it opened because of rising rent. This deepened my dad's resentment. From then on, it seemed like he drank even more.

Marlboros & Crown Royal. 1990s, Koreatown, L.A.

Not every memory I have of my father is rooted in neglect or abuse. You know the famous photos of those rooftop Koreans at California Market during the L.A. riots? That nineties ahjussi look was my dad's style back then. He'd wear a collared polo shirt tucked deep into his pants, with the poofy hairstyle that most Korean men his age rocked in that era. He smoked Marlboro Reds and Lights; each pack came with "miles" you could collect and redeem for branded items. My dad smoked so many damn Marlboros that we were able to procure a Marlboro bike, a Marlboro sleeping bag, and a bunch of other goods that we never ended up using.

His other favorite brand? Crown Royal. He drank the Canadian whisky daily, on the rocks or occasionally mixed with water. The bottles were a constant in our household, each empty purple velvet bag a reminder of his nightly ritual. I would keep my Pogs and slammers in them, and they eventually became storage for my Pokémon cards. I still feel traumatized thinking about the first time I tried the brown liquor when I was young—my virginal sip of alcohol. I was curious because I'd seen so many Crown Royal bottles. Like, what *was* this stuff? Well, unsurprisingly, I almost hurled after one sip. Never again.

To my dad, I wasn't entirely useless. Even in his frustration, he seemed to think I had one purpose: to be his delivery boy. As a little kid, I'd get sent to the liquor store to fetch cigarettes. All I had to say was "It's for my dad," and the cashier never questioned why a tiny

Korean boy in a ludicrously oversized graphic tee was purchasing a pack of Marlboros. Sometimes, Dad and I would pull up to some Koreatown strip mall, and he'd leave his green Buick Regal running, Radio Korea on the dial, while I dashed into different stores to grab him things. One frequent stop was Hanbat restaurant, on Western Avenue and 5th Street, where I'd grab two containers of seolleong-tang in a plastic bag, carefully balancing them both beneath a folded Korean newspaper. Then I'd pop into the video rental place next door to grab a dozen VHS tapes of the Korean variety shows and dramas my mom and he watched. This was the precursor to the Korean hallyu wave that would take over the world decades later. I don't even know how these rental places got away with producing shelf after shelf of bootlegged Korean programming. If you're a Korean American my age, surely you had something similar in your local market.

The happiest memories I have of my father are of us watching TV together. Not those Korean VHS tapes, but live sports. It wasn't exactly father–son bonding, but in those moments, he at least tolerated my presence. We'd watch the Chicago Bulls together, and that always put him in a good mood. How could it not? We were watching Michael Jordan in his prime! Koreans loved MJ, even in Lakertown. Seeing my dad get excited over Jordan's athletic feats got me pumped up, and next thing you know, we'd be sitting next to each other in matching Jordan Bulls jerseys. We'd watch Lakers games together too. Nick Van Exel, Vlade Divac, Elden Campbell—names that I can still reel off to this day, even though I barely keep up with the NBA now. Maybe my dad liked Michael Jordan so much because his name was easier to pronounce than anyone in the Lakers' lineup.

If my dad wasn't cheering a Jordan dunk, he was watching Tiger

Woods play golf. My mind can immediately conjure the image of Tiger onscreen, swinging away in his iconic red shirt. Watching Jordan and Tiger all the time might explain why my dad had such high standards for his kids. Their greatness distracted him from everything else.

Laughter was another way in which we connected. Anytime I could get my dad to crack up was a win. I'd run into his closet, put on a blazer and suit pants, hop in front of the TV, and act like a kid version of Bob Saget hosting *America's Funniest Home Videos*. Or I'd do some silly dance while pretending to be Michael Jackson. Most of the time he'd get pissed—"Get out of the way, I'm trying to watch TV!"—but once in a while I'd earn a chuckle. When I got him to smile, it felt so good, this validation from my own father. Attention became an obsession, my first addiction. I loved having it. I was a spotlight chaser, even back then.

Like many Asian parents, my dad tried to make sure my sister and I got good grades. Except it felt like he did it to keep up with other Korean families, not because he actually cared about furthering our education. For example, he heard other parents were buying *World Book* encyclopedias for their kids, and so he bought a set and just threw it in my room without explanation. I barely leafed through a single volume. Then came the computer. I used to walk to the Pio Pico public library to surf the net until one day my dad brought home a Dell desktop, almost as a flex. I wish I could say I used it for educational purposes, but it was more like sex ed. Streaming porn on a 56k dial-up was like snail mail, so I downloaded horny album skits on MP3 from Dr. Dre's *2001* and Biggie's *Ready to Die*. I'd put on headphones, close my eyes, and jerk off to the audio. (I can't be the only one . . . can I?) One time when I was around thirteen, my mom walked in on me with a plate of cut-up apples with toothpicks in them—classic Asian mom snack—only to be greeted by her son with his shorts down to his ankles. She ran out of the room, fruit strewn across my bedroom floor. (I'm sorry, Mama. *Eminem voice*)

Regardless of my dad's attempts to enhance my learning, I'd come home with terrible grades. And because of them, he'd periodically whoop my ass. His favorite tool to beat me with was this long plastic shoehorn that seemed aerodynamically designed to cut through air. That thing stung like a motherfucker. I joke now that I was raised like an old Panasonic TV: When something was wrong with it, you hit that shit instead of checking the manual to figure out what was wrong. Good parenting is reading the damn manual.

I may have been underachieving in school, but he was to blame too. He wasn't checking on my progress or instilling any lessons on why education was important. I became bitter about trying to meet expectations that never seemed clear.

But all that was nothing compared to how he treated my mom.

Mike Piazza. 1997, Koreatown, L.A.

I was able to avoid my father's K-rage simply by staying outside our apartment or locked inside my room. He only got pissed at me when I was in his line of vision. My mother, on the other hand, had to do actual business with him at the stores, and, oh yeah, raise two kids with him. She couldn't hide.

I knew my dad was a volatile guy, but I didn't realize the depth of his abuse of my mom until much later. She once told me that she'd hide the kitchen knives under the sink before going to bed, not because she thought he was necessarily the kind of person who would stab his wife in her sleep, but because she was scared of his temper. Growing up, I felt like a fly on the wall, seeing things my parents didn't think I was picking up. I'd strain to listen and to peek around corners, trying to tune into the state of their relationship. I was spying on my own family, eavesdropping through stairway rails and walls. I kept what I heard and saw to myself; Natalia was even less emotionally equipped to deal with what was happening. What I remember most often is my mom crying because of my dad's random cruelty. The mental toll was often worse than the occasional physical violence.

She might be cooking in the kitchen, and he'd yell, "You idiot!" at her for no reason. If she replied, "I'm not doing anything," he'd snap back, "How dare you talk back to me?" and possibly slap her.

When he came home drunk, he was angrier. He'd wake us all up in the middle of the night and ask nonsensical questions. If we didn't answer, he'd yell at us for not responding.

My mom would say, "I have to go to work tomorrow. I'm too tired. Can we talk later?"

Then he'd scream at her for talking back. Whatever burdens frustrated him outside the home caused him to lash out at us inside it.

One memory stands out more than most: the night when the volcano that had been rumbling for ages finally erupted. I was eleven and my sister was nine. My mom had gone to 24 Hour Fitness to work off some stress, leaving us with a neighbor, an older single woman. Afterward, my mom took a taxi home, where my dad lay waiting.

When she entered our apartment, he immediately bombarded her with accusations.

"Where were you? Who was the guy that dropped you off?" Infuriated, he started hitting her, covering her mouth so she couldn't breathe.

By this time, I was back home to witness the terror.

We lived on the third floor, and my mom ran out to the balcony, climbed onto the railing, and screamed, "I'm going to die!"

Her frantic desperation left me frozen in place. I was terrified. She came back in and dashed toward the apartment door. At this point, I was yelling at my dad to calm down. Just as she was about to escape, he caught her and slammed her head into the open door. My mom, dazed into a kind of zombie-like shock, steadied herself and stumbled out of our apartment. I found the phone and called 911.

The police arrived; my mother and I met them in the lobby. I was shaken, riding the apartment elevator with a police officer who looked kind of like the blond white guy from the show *CHiPs*. He peered down at me, a traumatized little Korean boy, pulled a Dodger trading card out of his pocket, and handed it to me. The player? Mike Piazza, whom I remember vividly because he got traded the next year.

The cops ended up asking my mom if they should take my dad in.

She replied wearily, "It's fine, just let it go."

After they left, my dad calmed down a little, but soon enough, he was back to yelling. My mom finally fled that night, staying with our neighbor for a while. For days after, my mom called to reassure me that she was doing fine—the saddest of phone calls—but couldn't return to the apartment yet. I had to answer these calls in secret because any time my dad was near, he'd try to snatch the phone and convince her to come back. Eventually, she did return, but it was a turning point in my parents' relationship. She had had enough.

When I reflect on my dad's reign of terror, I often see it through my mom's eyes in those moments. To this day, decades later, my mom struggles with high anxiety, paranoia, and fear of the things my dad put her through. As an adult, I get angry at her sometimes over nothing, and it scares me. The way she acts triggers me because I see a woman who endured so much from my dad, and I don't want to treat her the way he did. She carries a battered woman's trauma around, like a rescued animal.

Can you blame her, though? My mom came to this country thinking my father would take care of our family. But the only thing dependable about him was his anger. She carried two babies across the US border, only to carry the weight of her husband's failures for decades after.

The Split. 1999, Koreatown, L.A.

Growing up in a struggling family while being surrounded by people with money pissed me off. I couldn't understand why we were broke when my parents worked in the same business as those richer folks. But it wasn't just about money. Why didn't my parents have a loving relationship? Why was my dad such an angry alcoholic? And why did my mom get swallowed up by his anger instead of focusing on us? Saying this may not be fair to her because she was going through so much, but I felt like my sister and I were left to fend for ourselves. Many Asian American memoirs and think pieces and kids' books in recent years include the obligatory "stinky lunch" story, the trauma of being bullied for the kimchi or pungent dish in their lunchbox. I don't have one because I never got one packed for me. I *wish* I had a stinky lunch story!

When my parents finally separated, it was right at the cusp of two major events in my life: starting my short-lived high school career, and discovering the battle-rap scene that would change everything. Initially, I was relieved that they separated (but never divorced), because it meant I wouldn't have to listen to them fight anymore. But when he moved out, and Natalia and I stayed with Mom, I quickly realized that things were only going to get bleaker. She was extremely depressed, and there was nothing her children could do about it. Because she counted on my dad to provide for us, my mom had to start back from the bottom. She worked briefly as a bartender at a seedy dive, then at a Korean market handing out samples—the lowest entry-level jobs imaginable in Ktown.

Our new apartment, a two-bedroom on Vermont Avenue that my dad was willing to cover the rent for to off-load his fatherly duties, looked like a storage unit that had exploded. The apartment floor was covered with books and other stuff she hoarded, to the point where you couldn't see the carpet. Similarly, the entire bathroom counter was filled with products. I can't believe we lived like that, but I understand now that my mom was really suffering. My dad's style was always clean and structured; he even threw away things I collected because he wanted to keep the apartment clean. Freed from those restrictions, my mom took it to the other extreme. I took advantage of the disorder by inviting my stoner friends over when my mom wasn't there. We'd smoke weed, eat up everything in the fridge, then retreat into my room for hours-long freestyle sessions.

That's how I lived when my parents split up. It was a tough time, but it allowed me to run loose around the city and do whatever I wanted. Even as a teen, I was partying past three in the morning. My mom would leave fifteen voice messages, and I'd ignore them all. My younger sister was being *extra* bad. Because my dad was rarely around, and even less so after they split, I had to be the father figure for my sister from a very young age. I tried to look out for her best interests, especially as she hit her teen years, but I was acting out already—and she was even wilder. She started hanging out with gangbangers and taggers, doing drugs, and routinely getting busted for shoplifting. I took drugs and misbehaved too, but I was doing it all while freestyling. Pretty soon, I was dedicating every waking hour to the art.

In Koreatown, I was an outcast. I hung out with a lot of poor KA kids, not the ones who moved to La Crescenta or Glendale. Some of them, whose parents were in dire straits like mine, went into crime and joined gangs; I somehow avoided that life. The kids from tough upbringings who ended up as criminals don't often get their stories shared. We hear a lot about the Forever 21 empire and other success stories, but nobody seems to care about the stories of Korean immigrants who came here and failed.

Over the years, not just my family but other downtown Korean families fell apart too—often due to dads who couldn't navigate their families through gambling debts or domestic turmoil. Some of the kids my dad once adored and compared me to didn't go to college or follow any passion, and are now themselves working downtown, pushing cardboard boxes like their dads once did. Compared to those downtown kids, I'm a success story, and so is my sister, who went from high school dropout to a master's grad. Look at us now. I guess all that parental disappointment paid off.

Father vs. Son. 2012, Koreatown, L.A.

I dropped a song in 2012, when I was twenty-six, called "Growing Young." It was the only way I could process my feelings about my dad.

Promised that I would never grow up and be him
But I never grew up at all
And now I'm womanizing and cheatin', drinkin' heavily in the p.m.
Having myself a monster's ball, just like my pa

Back then, I was making a lot of excuses for my bad behavior—especially in relationships—by blaming it on my upbringing. I felt like an asshole because I couldn't break the cycle. Even when I started making music and winning big battles, I never told my dad. What was the point of impressing him? In my midtwenties, when I was living alone and finally making money, my dad would sometimes drunk dial me randomly and blurt out, "I love you, Jonnie." Even though he was clearly intoxicated and possibly just bragging about me to his drinking buddies, it felt like he wanted me to know he was proud of me.

On one such call, he surprised me. "Why don't you come over to where I'm at?"

He'd never asked me to join him at a bar before. So, I went. It turned out to be a Koreatown "hostess" bar—the kind where aging men pay for young women to pour them drinks and fawn over them.

My dad was in high spirits. Surrounded by friends and bar girls, he proudly introduced me: "This is my son."

The women batted their eyes, telling me, "Oh, you look just like him, so good-looking," gassing me up.

At home, my dad's mood had been either rage or silence. Out here, he seemed like a harmless, hilarious guy. It was jarring. In this social setting, he played the happy drunk who broke the ice by dancing or singing karaoke. For the first time, I saw how my mom must've seen him back in Argentina: a cocky, charming big talker. My dad told everyone that I was a rapper, and they looked at me in awe. I could tell by how the women interacted with him that he was a regular.

So there I was, drinking next to a surreal, fun-loving version of my dad that I'd never known before. His friends, the bartender, the hostesses—they all loved him. He worked the room, chatting up his buddies and ordering the girls, "Pour my son a shot." Wait, was my dad . . . kind of *cool*? He was a ladies' man, cracking jokes, getting loose. We were bonding, having good conversation, when suddenly, he slurred out a drunken apology. "Jonnie, I know I messed up, but you turned out fine." His lip quivered, like he might cry. And for a second, I believed him. I forgot about the spoon test. I forgot about the beatings and all the messed-up shit he'd done.

I went home and life continued on. It took years before I stopped fearing him. It wasn't until I was financially stable enough to support not only myself but also my mom that I finally felt allowed to think: *Fuck my dad.* Even so, it's tough to not feel sorry for him now. He still lives in Koreatown and mostly takes care of himself, but calls me from time to time to ask sheepishly for money. He usually positions it as a short-term loan but never pays me back. I don't see him as terrifying anymore or cool like that one night in Koreatown. I see him as sad. Powerless. A broken dream in the flesh.

When he's sober, Dad will brush off the past with lines like,

"That's over. You gotta get over it and work." He never takes real accountability. Or he'll spread the blame: "Me and your mom both messed up, but now it's up to you. I can't do anything for you." That much is true. He also tells me to never get married, and so far, that's one piece of advice I've followed. My mom still apologizes to me to this day, and honestly, I'm tired of hearing it. That's one thing I can agree with my dad on: It *is* too late for apologies. What good does an apology do me now? It is what it is. I doubt my father and I will ever break new ground. Call that pessimistic, but it's not uncommon for boomer Korean dads and their adult KA sons. The pattern is usually the same: A hard immigrant life leads to negligence or abuse, which breeds lifelong resentment. The language barrier and a refusal to acknowledge the past keep that resentment from ever being resolved. It's unfortunate, but I've made my peace with it.

In the end, I thank my dad for a few things, for better or for worse. He's the origin of my pettiness and competitiveness, which can be unhealthy, but made me lethal in battle rap. Like him, I can detach and shut down when problems arise, like a computer stuck with a spinning pinwheel. It's ironic that I became a battle rapper, because I never liked confrontation in real life. In his way, my dad didn't either. He'd just explode and get violent so he wouldn't have to deal with it. I moved in the opposite direction. When things got heated, I used humor to defuse tension. Words became my weapons. Punchlines, not punches. If I attacked someone, it wasn't to hurt them—it was to make everybody else laugh at them with me.

But I couldn't learn those lessons at home. The household was too volatile. I had to find a place where wit mattered more than fists. A safe space—well, relatively safe, anyway—where I could experience confrontation without violence. If my parents had been paying attention, they might've kept me from ever finding this sanctuary. But they weren't. Before that, though, I had to make some mistakes on my own.

THE APPLE NEVER FALLS TOO FAR FROM THE TREE,

UNLESS THE TREE STAYS AT THE KARAOKE BAR UNTIL 3.

I DON'T KNOW WHAT WAS HARDER TO SEE: YOUR DRUNK ASS ON THE CARPET ASLEEP,

OR THE WAY MY MOM USED TO CRY ONCE YOU STARTED TO CHEAT,

EVEN THOUGH SHE STAYED, SHE ALWAYS WORE HER HEART ON HER SLEEVE.

Battle: "Father vs. Son"
Art by Michelle Kwon

NOW THERE'S SEAWEED SOUP AND KIMCHI JUICE SPLATTERED ON THE WALL LIKE BLOOD- YOU'LL SEE THE STAIN FOREVER NO MATTER HOW LONG YOU SCRUB.

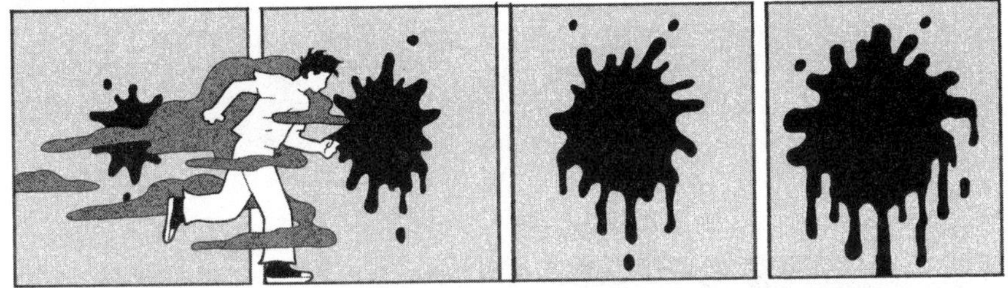

YOU PLAYED GOLF EVERY WEEK, BUT NEVER BROUGHT ME ONCE,

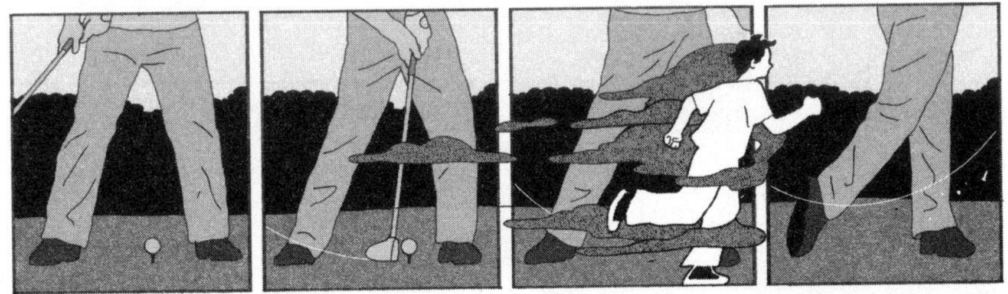

AND FORGOT MY BIRTHDAY BUT NEVER FORGOT YOUR CLUBS.

WHILE YOU WERE READING THE KOREAN NEWSPAPER RIGHT UNDER YOUR NOSE,

성일보

I WAS ON THE COVER AT 16 FOR DOING HUNDREDS OF SHOWS.

NOW YOUR SON'S ON THE ROAD, WENT FROM LONDON TO SEOUL...

'CAUSE IN SOME FUCKED-UP, BEAUTIFUL WAY, I'M JUST A PRODUCT OF YOU.

CHAPTER TWO

THE BLUNDER YEARS

Dumb First, Dead Last

In 1998, I was on the cusp of adolescence. My family was still intact but wouldn't be for long; and I was teetering on the line between childhood innocence and teenage chaos. Three pivotal moments happened to me that year, when I was twelve years old, that shaped the next stage of my life: The first time I stood in front of a camera. The first time I got high. And the first time I fell in love with hip-hop. Those moments didn't feel connected to each other back then, but now I realize that they foreshadowed what was to come in my teen years: the courage to perform, the desire to escape, and the need to master a craft. The randomness of it all was a sign too. It was the year I embraced freestyling as a way of life.

D-List Child Star

I'm sitting on a couch next to a couple of multiculti kids playing PlayStation when *bam*, we get sucked into the TV and dropped straight into the game, turning into bomb-wielding robot versions of ourselves.

Was it a dream? Yeah, kinda. But it was also real. Because when I was twelve, I starred in my first TV commercial: a spot for the PS1 game *Bomberman World*. For a minute, I really thought I might become a child star. Growing up in the 1990s as a latchkey kid, I was raised on sitcoms, where wisecracking children always drew the biggest laughs. I wanted that in real life, but my household was about as funny as a "Very Special Episode" about alcoholism. So, I got the itch to be in TV and film. I looked up to Filipino American actor Dante Basco, aka Rufio from *Hook*, aka the most swagged-out Asian I had ever seen. Living in the epicenter of the industry made stardom feel like an attainable dream.

My mom was supportive of my Hollywood fantasies, which was unsurprising since she fancied herself a performer as well. She nicknamed me Johny Tolengo, after a flashy character from a 1980s Argentine comedy. She told me later, "You were never destined to be a model student, but I always knew you could be an entertainer." She took me to get professional headshots taken when I was little. In L.A., we were surrounded by billboards and radio ads for companies, some sketchier than others, that targeted would-be child stars and their families, promising acting classes, agent meetings, and a shortcut to fame. Anytime I caught wind of an ad, I'd write down the details and beg my mom to take me.

Even a regular shopping trip could turn into a chance for a big break. I signed myself up for a casting call at the Beverly Center when I was eleven and somehow landed my first audition. I walked into a room where two people sat smiling behind a camera. In front of them was a chair and a video-game console. All I had to do was sit down and pretend to play. Little did they know that I barely ever played video games—my parents were too cheap to buy me a console—and I got booked for the gig.

My mom came with me to the all-day shoot. The only clear memory I have, other than having to don a bulky robot suit for the IRL-to-video-game part, was that the makeup artist said she was surprised I didn't need chopsticks to eat the catering. An awkward silence ensued, my face burning. Even then, I knew exactly why I was being singled out for that comment. Yay, my first Hollywood microaggression.

After the *Bomberman* commercial made it to TV, I got my first hit of the limelight and loved it. Soon after, Natalia and I starred in a local Korean TV ad for a business called Computer Ahnex, singing their catchy jingle. I was then asked to try out for a recurring role on a Fox Kids program, which could've been my breakthrough—but I missed a deadline in the casting process. My mom pleaded with them to extend it, but I still got left out. And that was my short-lived run as a child actor. Ironically, I continued following a common child-star trajectory, because not long after that, I discovered drugs.

Palm Springs Was a Trip

I tried acid before I smoked my first cigarette—well, actually, I got my first taste of both on the same day in 1998. My family wasn't the vacationing type, but every now and then we'd take a day trip on a

Korean gwangwang tour bus to somewhere within driving distance of L.A. It wasn't exactly a jaunt through Europe, but it was still a treat to get out of the city once in a while. On this particular excursion to Palm Springs, my parents took my sister and me to join other Korean families who worked downtown in the jaba business.

The adults sat in the front of the bus, while the kids gathered in the back. Among them were two girls my age, Crystal and Yuna, both twelve. We were at that stage when we were getting curious about high school, life after puberty, and whatever it was that made teenagers seem cool. Which made the fifteen-year-old boy with us (we'll call him Jimmy) a natural ringleader. Jimmy wore a beaded necklace and jumbo JNCO jeans that would fit over my torso. He carried around glow sticks—at fifteen, he was already heavily into the rave scene. We sat there, wide-eyed, listening to his stories about sneaking out for drug-fueled all-nighters at warehouses across the city. *So, this is what teenage life has in store,* I thought greedily.

About halfway into the two-hour drive, Jimmy reached into his pocket and pulled out a crumpled ball of aluminum foil. Inside were four tiny tabs, each marked with a picture of a Smurf. He looked at Crystal, Yuna, and me and solemnly pointed to his hand.

"This is acid," he said. He slid each of us a tab. "Put this under your tongue and let it dissolve," he whispered. "And whatever you do, don't swallow."

We looked at each other and smiled. You'd think we'd be more nervous under peer pressure, but it felt weirdly safe, like a supervised experiment. We were all in this together. Without hesitation, we ingested the acid as instructed. I waited for something to happen. It had no taste whatsoever, and I wasn't sure what I was supposed to feel or how long it took to kick in. I just stared out the window as the bus rumbled east along Interstate 10.

Thirty or so minutes passed without incident. Then, Crystal started giggling. I glanced over at Yuna, and she was laughing too. Suddenly, we were all cracking up, loudly and uncontrollably, Jimmy included. Everything was hilarious; even the singsong drone of our parents' chatter, usually so annoying, felt like comedy. The colors of the landscape along the I-10, once muted and unexciting, started to glow. The endless spin of the wind turbines outside grew hypnotic. As Jimmy proudly showed off his glow-stick moves, I suddenly understood why they were rave essentials. Nothing seemed real. I was floating just outside the bullshit of ordinary life, and it felt great.

Our laughter grew louder and louder, which set off a minor panic. Were the adults going to figure out that we were on drugs? Jimmy started to hush us, paranoid that we might tell on him. Of course, being Korean parents, they were completely oblivious. Rather than being suspicious, our parents seemed amused at how well their kids were getting along. Jimmy's mom started bragging to the other parents about her son's dance moves—"Show them that spinny thing you do with the sticks!"—which made us laugh harder.

At some point, we made it to Palm Springs. We gathered in a park for a classic Korean-style picnic: L.A. galbi lifted straight off the grill onto white paper plates with a side of japchae and eaten with wooden chopsticks. After the meal, most of the parents wandered off to soak in the local hot springs, the ones that smell like rotten eggs. Don't ask me what happened next, because I couldn't tell you. All I recall is the descent back to reality.

Once we were out of sight from the parental pack, Jimmy handed me a Marlboro Light. "It'll help," he said.

That's how I smoked my first cigarette, in the fetal position on some park grass, to come down from my first acid trip. I wouldn't try LSD again for another four years, but by then I was a high school stoner, down to try anything that helped me feel numb and escape. My twelve-year-old mind didn't process it then, but looking back, I think acid unlocked a part of my brain that I didn't know existed.

I never saw Jimmy again. Once in a while, I'll randomly cross paths with Crystal or Yuna in Ktown. They're now married with children. We'll smile, shake our heads, and say, "Remember Palm Springs?" I guess you could say it was all a PLUR.

Out of My Element

By age twelve, many Korean kids in my neighborhood were going to after-school hagwons, the Kumon-like tutoring facilities that were ubiquitous in Korea and quickly catching on in Ktown. My parents sent my sister and me to one, but only briefly. I think my dad figured it was a waste of money once he saw our grades weren't getting any better.

That meant our after-school hours were totally free. One afternoon, while walking home from the school bus stop, Natalia and I noticed a group of youngins walking into a church-like brick building. The way they were moving—almost skipping, not trudging along—suggested that they were headed somewhere fun. But wait, it *was* a place of worship: the Los Angeles First Church of the Nazarene. Why would kids be rushing into church after school? On a whim, we stepped inside after them. Following their voices to the third floor, we discovered something called the Bresee Youth Center, established in 1987 by a foundation named after Phineas Franklin Bresee, the pastor who opened the Church of the Nazarene in L.A. in 1895. The youth program was basically a Boys & Girls Club for inner-city kids. I glanced around and saw that my sister and I were the only Asians in a room full of Latino and Black children.

Though Bresee was started by a church, it didn't feel like one. I saw a couple kids setting up balls at a pool table and others stationed at a row of cheap computers. There were tables in the center where adults sat helping students with their homework. A hum of carefree banter bounced off the walls. It was clearly a low-budget operation, but the vibe inside fit the religious location: friendly, nonjudgmental, and inviting. From that day forward, Nat and I turned Bresee into our own hagwon. In place of our disinterested parents, Bresee became the first of several community organizations that helped raise us. The other children in the program and I formed a little crew, a bunch of minorities from the hood talking trash, killing time, and figuring out life together. As always, I embraced the novelty of my sis and me being the only Asian American kids around. Beyond the games and activities they set up for us, the staff became supportive mentors—not quite parental figures, but close enough to matter. There was an old Jewish film buff named Jerold who used to work at Warner Brothers. A curmudgeonly old-timer who favored a fedora and suspenders, he introduced me to Buster Keaton, the Marx Brothers, and classic movies like *The French Connection* and *Taxi Driver.* What he taught me about shooting and editing sparked my interest in film, which carried over into my career when I started making music videos. I also became close with a hippie-looking white guy with a ponytail named Seth, the education coordinator at the time (and Bresee's executive director today). He also rapped as a hobby, except he did so while strumming an acoustic guitar, which is about as white as rapping gets. Fresh out of UCLA, Seth felt more like an older homie than a teacher, which is probably why I felt more motivated to stay on my studies under his guidance. So I could impress big bro.

My parents were only vaguely aware of what we were up to at Bresee, but they were just glad we weren't out in the streets. During the summer, Bresee would send us to an overnight camp usually reserved for rich white kids through a scholarship like the Fresh Air Fund. For a week, we'd go zip-lining, swim, and play paintball on a picturesque campsite—all for free. When I brought home the permission slip, my mom signed without even reading it. Any paper with paragraphs of uninterrupted English gave my parents a headache, so the skim-and-sign was standard procedure in my household.

When Bresee launched a hip-hop program, it was my first exposure to the history of the culture. Sure, I loved the Snoop songs blaring from the boomboxes next to my father's store, but that's about all I knew. What I learned was that rap was only one of four elements of hip-hop, alongside breakdancing, DJing, and graffiti. I eagerly dove in.

Nat immediately gravitated toward breaking and figured out how to pop and lock in her first class. Once I hit the floor to bust a move, my fragile, inflexible ass didn't stand a chance. Graffiti seemed cool, so I adopted the tag name MICRO and started toting around markers and a little black book to practice. One day, on the city bus, I was doodling in my book when a dude pulled up next to me and asked me what my tag was. As it turned out, he also tagged MICRO, and when he showed me *his* black book—with intricate, mural-worthy MICRO tags everywhere—I knew that I couldn't hang. (At fifteen, I got arrested for graffiti, and then it was truly a wrap for me. Dodging cops didn't seem like a fun pastime.) I took a stab at DJing on my friend's used Stanton starter kit, but my hands were so clumsy, it felt like I was mixing with Mickey Mouse gloves on.

One by one, I tried and failed at all the elements of hip-hop, which left one thing: rap. How fitting that this trial-and-error approach—picking up stuff and seeing what stuck—led me there since that is the essence of a freestyle. A few years later, I found another youth program called J.U.i.C.E. (Justice by Uniting in Creative Energy). It was held every Wednesday afternoon, led by a headwrap-wearing Mexican American dancer from Chicago named Lady Sol. Her credentials were impressive, having performed with the likes of Busta Rhymes and Lauryn Hill. She was a hip-hop encyclopedia; she taught us about rap's origins in the Bronx, introducing names I'd never heard before: Kool Herc, Grandmaster Flash, and KRS-One. Mind you, my favorite music video at the time was Nelly's "Tip Drill," so spicy and thong-heavy it could only be aired late night on *BET Uncut*.

I began nerding out on the lore and stopped wearing do-rags. (Yes, I had a brief do-rag phase.) I learned American history, the stuff they conveniently left out of school: the prison industrial complex, police brutality, and the crack epidemic. If my initial phase of embracing hip-hop was soaking it in as a fan, and the third phase was participating as a rapper, then this middle phase was about studying hip-hop—an education that separated appreciation from appropriation.

J.U.i.C.E. held classes for each element of hip-hop taught by OG mentors: Mark Luv from the Zulu Nation taught DJing; Easy Roc from Rock Steady Crew and Poppin' Chuck were the breakdance instructors; Cre8 worked with aspiring graffiti artists; and spoken-word rappers GaKnew and Brutha Gimel from Da Poetry Lounge shepherded the young MCs, including me. We had writing workshops where we scribbled down rhymes over beats. GaKnew prodded me to dabble in slam poetry, which felt like rap's nerdy cousin—a skill that helped me later on in a cappella battles. The experience I gained at J.U.i.C.E. set the stage for what came next. I was getting to the age where I needed to experience rap in its rawest form.

But first, I had to survive high school. Spoiler alert: I didn't.

Chronic Underachiever

Freshman year at John Marshall High started the same way nearly every day: Before the homeroom bell each morning, I met up with the homies in front of the building, and we immediately bounced. Everybody still called me Chino, so in classic 2000s fashion, I was wearing a trucker hat with "Chino" tagged in graffiti across the front. My crew included Latino skaters, punk rockers, and underground hip-hop heads. We rocked skate tees, Dickies shorts, and backpacks with band patches for Nirvana, 311, Wu-Tang Clan, and Sublime. Musical tastes varied, but we had one thing in common: We were stoners.

Our days were about nothing but getting high. The daily mission was to score a bag of weed and find a place to smoke it. That entailed a lot of trooping around Los Feliz and calling up different plugs we knew. Bingo. Someone snagged a gram of chronic for about twenty bucks, and we were off to a friend's garage, a dead-end street, or, if we were lucky, my vacant apartment. If nobody had anything to roll with, we'd get MacGyver with it and use a soda can, or better yet, an apple to smoke out of. Poked a couple holes, packed a bowl where the stalk was, and voilà. Finally, we lit up, passed it around, and started rhyming on the spot. The pot neutralized any tendency to second-guess myself. The mental roadblock of inhibition was gone. Words flowed out of me, anxiety-free. Then, around three p.m., we dapped each other up and dispersed. Another successful day of school in the books.

My first high school wasn't actually John Marshall. I started ninth grade at Belmont Senior High, close to downtown L.A., the school I was assigned to based on my home address. I was one of maybe six Asians at Belmont; the others were straight FOBs, "fresh off the boat" Asians who barely spoke English. The vast majority of the student population was Latino. Belmont was your typical hood school—the kind with pregnant freshmen and teenagers with "MS-13" tatted across their necks. It was like the school from the movie *Dangerous Minds*, except I don't think Michelle Pfeiffer would've made it a week there. I barely made it a semester.

I transferred to John Marshall midway through my freshman year. (We used the zip code of my mom's friend's place to finesse the transfer.) In Los Feliz, close to Silver Lake and Echo Park—the trinity of cool L.A. neighborhoods—John Marshall is the alma mater of will.i.am, Judge Lance Ito, Kansas City Chiefs coach Andy Reid, and some dude you may have heard of named Leonardo DiCaprio. The school was still predominantly Latino, but much more diverse, with white, Black, and Asian American students. Some of my classmates were sons and daughters of directors and musicians; Flea from Red

Hot Chili Peppers had a music school down the street. Now this was more like it.

But be careful what you wish for. I had escaped a hood school for an artsier one, and likewise graduated to harder drugs—ecstasy, mushrooms, cocaine, and even meth. The artsy kids knew how to get fucked up. To top it off, the herb was stronger there too. Chronic and higher-grade pot replaced the weak shwag I was smoking at Belmont. Then kush came into the mix and changed the game. The buds resembled a science experiment, glowing with crystals and red hairs. My first bong rip sent me straight to the moon.

By this time, my mom was catching me smoking at the house, but there wasn't much she could do about it. One time, she walked into my room at the exact moment I was hitting the bong, my face buried in the glass mouthpiece. She flipped out, ripping the bong out of my hands, and raised it over her head like she was about to smash it.

I held my hands up. "Mom, Mom, hold on—that thing cost me eighty bucks!"

She paused, and I could see the mental math all over her face. Putting the bong down, she sighed and walked out of my room. Her son smoking weed was bad, but wasting money was worse.

I began experimenting beyond marijuana with psychedelics and coke. Meth started becoming a thing. I don't recall exactly how it infiltrated my school, but it spread quickly, and out of nowhere, a whole swath of students got addicted. I had a lot of Filipino homies who smoked it. Back then, we naively thought meth was just another drug among the many that were on hand, only more potent. *Intervention* wasn't on TV yet, and there were no cautionary online videos or "This is what you'll look like on meth in twenty years" posters. I saw friends' whole personalities change after becoming meth addicts, from fun-loving to foaming at the mouth. One even stole money from my house; I took the ass whooping from my dad on his behalf. Thank God I never got hooked.

The John Marshall community extended into Silver Lake, where I would go to house parties and see the likes of Shia LaBeouf and Lindsay Lohan turn up. Former child stars I had watched on Disney Channel were going ham on drugs. It wasn't hard to see why kid actors often ended up trainwrecks—everything was readily available to them, and in abundance, with no adult supervision. It was at one of these Silver Lake shindigs my freshman year that I lost my virginity. We had gathered at the home of a rich white kid named Beau—what other kind of kid would be named Beau?—whose father was a director. Dad must've had a few bangers, because their house was huge. Everyone inside was drinking from handles of Jose Cuervo and forty ounces of Mickey's. My tolerance for alcohol was much lower than for weed—I also weighed maybe a buck and change—so I got super drunk, super fast.

I started making out with a mixed-race Black-white girl in the hallway. She was a senior, and I was a freshman, so it was obvious who was captaining that ship. Next thing you know, she grabbed my arm and led me to one of the many rooms in that palatial home. *Oh shit, we're about to fuck,* I thought. Everything else happened pretty fast. The scene played like your classic teen comedy: I fished out a condom from my wallet, put it on, lay with her . . . and three strokes later, busted a nut. I rolled over, almost in shock. *Oh shit, I'm not a virgin anymore.*

I returned to the party feeling like the man, but my pride was short-lived. Come to find out, I wasn't the first guy she had sex with at that party. Back at school, my nickname for the rest of the year was "Sloppy Seconds." Embarrassing for me, but undoubtedly more so for her, since at least I got to lose my V-card. That breakthrough didn't turn me into a ladies' man, however. I was still a scrawny Asian stoner with no game and no rap persona to lean on as a crutch.

I've made it this far into my high school story without once mentioning actual school. What is there to say? Until I dropped out, I was the student who raised his hand during a lecture just to get in a wisecrack. Teachers would get annoyed, but they also saw something in me. I'll never forget when my sixth-grade teacher said, "Jonnie, you're brimming with creative potential. You just use it in all the wrong ways." By sophomore year, I wasn't using it at all, at least for academics. I had no premeditated plan to drop out; it just slowly happened in the tenth grade. I'd skip a couple days a week, then a couple more, and eventually I stopped going altogether. At some point, I realized that I had ditched school so many times that even if I returned, I would be forced into an extra year to make up all the failed classes. A super senior? Couldn't be me. And it's not like I dropped out because I knew I wanted to dedicate my life to rapping. My only goal was to mess around and smoke weed with my friends. In reality, I was depressed too. My parents were splitting up, and the future seemed bleak. I don't remember this, but my mom told me later that I would sometimes sit in my room and cry. Somehow, I've blocked that memory.

You'd think one of my parents would have forced me to go back to school or at least talked some sense into me, but they were so caught up in their own stuff that they didn't even know. I would get up in the morning, leave the house like I was going to school, and then chill somewhere until the early evening. This went on for two full years, and by the end of it, my little sister had dropped out of high school too. In retrospect, maybe my parents *did* know that I wasn't going to school—or at least my mom did—and either didn't care or were too defeated to do anything about it. That might be even sadder. With no hope for a degree, I had to figure out how to make money somehow, some way.

Wage Against the Machine

When I turned nineteen, a friend got me a job as a bail bondsman. Getting certified for the job was about as easy as getting a driver's license. You just had to be eighteen or older with a clean record. Do a few days of training, take the licensing exam, and boom—you're official. It was a sleazy job and a tough grind, straight out of Quentin Tarantino's *Jackie Brown*. Our office targeted Koreans locked up for domestic violence and DUIs—common crimes for ahjussis in Ktown. We'd comb through the L.A. County Sheriff's Department website, searching arrest records for any "Kim," "Lee," or "Park." Then, we'd solicit jails, and I'd be sent in to interview the recent inmates through the glass. Nearly all were Korean immigrants who were shaken up being behind bars—confused, scared, with little understanding of the American legal system. I'd recite the company line: "Get bailed out now. It'll look better to the judge." They were in no position to decline. One time, I was sitting across from a grizzled Korean guy who stared at me quizzically. "Oh, Jonnie?" he said. It was one of my dad's buddies from downtown. Not long after that, I quit.

That bail-bond job was notable because it was the only place I worked that I didn't scam. I'm not proud of that fact, but here's my excuse: I watched my parents work so hard for so little that I was determined not to be a sucker for Uncle Sam. Even before I had a proper job, the hustler's spirit was within me.

Bresee had a system in which they doled out points for completing homework assignments. Kids could then exchange those rewards for snacks and prizes. Rack up enough, and you might even win a Nintendo Game Boy. Well, I found a back door into the system and loaded up on free points. For three years, I used them to stockpile snacks and Game Boys, which I would then peddle to the homies. When my scheme was discovered, I got kicked out of Bresee. (The shame dogged me for years until I made enough to donate money back to the organization.) In middle school, I sold illegally downloaded CDs (to students *and* teachers) and used Photoshop to create counterfeit Metro student bus passes. All of this was merely foreshadowing what was to come in my teenage years.

When I dropped out of high school, I worked a litany of shitty jobs that became slightly less shitty because I was stealing from them. If you've ever suffered through an entry-level, dead-end gig, you know the feeling: Grind for two weeks, get that paycheck, and then stare at the pitiful number like, *That's it?* So, to make it more equitable, I skimmed off the top. If I was going to get paid crumbs, the least I could do was sneak some bread on the side.

First, it was at Jamba Juice, where I was running my own rewards program at the register. I ratcheted things up a notch when the Grove shopping center opened, and I got a job at Pacific Theatres. Once again, I tapped the till, this time at the concessions stand, which we all know is stupid overpriced. A customer would fork over twenty dollars for a large popcorn and large soda; I'd press the fifty-cent Extra Cheese button and pocket the $19.50 in, uh, extra cheese. On a busy weekend shift, I could make $800 easy, sometimes even a four-digit cut. By the end of summer, I had enough loot saved to buy my first car, a used silver Ford Focus. (This is the vehicle I drove to some of my most famous battles.) I was bringing in so much dough that I would throw parties for my coworkers.

Eventually I got fired—not for stealing, but for always being late. That's what pissed me off the most, that my money train got derailed for the dumbest reason imaginable. My next job was at a vegetarian spot called M Café on Melrose and La Brea, where celebrities like Alicia Silverstone, Zack de la Rocha, and André 3000 would routinely pull up. I ran the same Pacific Theatres maneuver at the café, but this one wasn't as lucrative or sustainable. For a brief spell, I was an usher at the Wiltern Theatre, where I'd take bribes to get people into the VIP section for concerts. (I had a full-circle moment when I performed there years later.)

My last "real" job came after the bail-bondsman experience. I got hired at a branch of Farmers Insurance run by a Korean family. They kept a template for proof-of-insurance papers in the office. So, for a very reasonable fee of $150, I would type in my friends' info and print out hard copies of fake insurance to present in case they got pulled over. That was a risky scam because getting caught could've meant a felony charge. After I got spooked about the consequences, I quit Farmers and transitioned into the struggle life of an aspiring rapper.

I'd like to say that all my grifts had entrepreneurial intent, but there was no plan or end goal. I just needed cash to keep my head above water. I've never lacked motivation to get money but failed to master the financial literacy to make it grow. Even though I'm much better with money now—thanks to advisers and accountants—I still get intimidated by contracts and avoid dealing with numbers. If it weren't for the cautionary tale of my parents' financial mistakes, I genuinely think I would not give a fuck about money the way I do. It's a blessing that I got out of the endless work grind when I did, because surely my luck was going to run out at some point. Let's just say it's a good thing rap became my full-time hustle.

CHAPTER THREE

BLOWED

Some of the greatest entertainers of our time have had sacred places to hone their skills. Dojos, if you will. Testing grounds where they pushed their limits alongside peers with similar ambitions, with the hope of becoming one of the GOATs. Safe but fiercely competitive spaces that helped unlock their full creative potential.

The Ramones, Blondie, and Talking Heads had CBGB in New York City. Richard Pryor, Robin Williams, and David Letterman had the Comedy Store on the Sunset Strip. Harry, Ron, and Hermione had Hogwarts.

And me? I had the Project Blowed open mic in South Central L.A.

Blowed was where I sharpened my lyrical sword, thickened my soft Asian skin, and put in my ten thousand hours of freestyling. It's where I became "Dumbfoundead" and met the crew who would ultimately become my chosen family.

Before my christening at Project Blowed, I'd already been rapping for a year, not yet recording music, but freestyling in my school cafeteria and at house parties. In those environments, all eyes were on me. You might as well have hung a sign around my neck that read "Will Rap for Drugs," because people would offer me party favors just to keep me flowing, like putting change into a jukebox. I remember rapping in a smoke-filled living room, surrounded by shrieks of approval. I'd freestyle for hours, dripping sweat, losing myself in the words. It was a spiritual experience. Rhyming was also my antidepressant, keeping my mind off family problems, even if what I was going through sometimes slipped into a rhyme.

Rock out with my cock out
Kicked out of my pop's house
I seen my momma gettin' knocked out like Pacquiao

My brain swapped personal trauma for rhyming couplets. Sitting in a car or bus, I'd look up at billboards and signs around the city and start stitching rhymes to whatever words I saw. If I passed an Olive Garden, my brain would spit out "Dolly Parton," "Macaulay Culkin," and so on. I deposited these rhymes into a mental word bank that I'd access in my next cypher. Little did I know that my hobby was about to become a lifelong obsession and career. Because in 2001, I stepped into the big leagues.

I first heard the words "Project Blowed" from a Filipino friend named James. The Filipinos usually put me onto the coolest hip-hop shit, as they'd already been dominating DJing and breakdancing. I called them the "gateway Asians" because they were often the first to venture off and integrate themselves into other cultures, while other Asians I knew tended to hang among themselves. When James told me about Project Blowed, it sounded like a top secret government experiment, like Area 51. It was an open-mic workshop in South Central L.A., where some of the top rappers in the city, and sometimes the entire country, showcased their skills. I was so cocky then that I didn't feel one bit nervous about going to Project Blowed for the first time. If anything, I was excited for the opportunity to destroy more rappers' egos the same way I was crushing kids in the cafeteria.

Fuck, was I wrong.

43rd & Leimert

Project Blowed went down every Thursday night at ten in Leimert Park, South Central, on the corner of West 43rd Place and Leimert Boulevard. For context, I lived on West 3rd Street at the time, more than forty blocks away. Most Asians never ventured south of Pico Boulevard unless they owned a liquor store or beauty shop in the hood. In the past, it wasn't a neighborhood I ventured out to on purpose. I had been missing out.

The Leimert area has long been a bastion of African American arts and activism, and Duke Ellington, Ella Fitzgerald, and Ray Charles once called it home. Over the years, people flocked there for its poetry and jazz bars, where legends like drummer Billy Higgins and pianist Horace Tapscott performed. During the 1970s and '80s, Leimert was known for its vibrant gay community. The richest of the rich lived just a block east, while the poorest of the poor were a block in the other direction. Into the 1990s and 2000s, active gangbangers from bordering hoods passed through the perimeter. Yet, across all classes and affiliations, arts and culture thrived in Leimert.

The legacy of Black artistry evolved into something new in 1994 with Project Blowed. Its roots could be traced back to the Good Life Café on Crenshaw Boulevard, where a generation of experimental MCs—masters of ceremonies, aka microphone controllers, aka rappers—began carving out their own scene at the start of the nineties. When Good Life closed, its creative spirit moved to a Leimert community center called KAOS Network. By then, L.A. gangsta rap had taken over the mainstream, with Dr. Dre and Snoop picking up the mantle from N.W.A and Ice-T. At Good Life, those conventions were subverted. In a neighborhood still reeling from the aftermath of the L.A. riots, Project Blowed pushed the art form in new directions.

KAOS was run by Ben Caldwell, an older African American filmmaker and activist since the 1960s, who opened his artist space for a weekly open mic. Project Blowed was where Freestyle Fellowship—Aceyalone, Myka9, P.E.A.C.E., and Self Jupiter, four of the coldest freestyle rappers you'll ever hear—laid their foundation.

A much less accomplished quartet headed to South Central for Blowed our first Thursday night: James, a big, nerdy Black kid named Jamal, a Mexican-Japanese skater named Robbie, and me. The four of us crammed into James's mom's beat-up Honda Civic and trekked to Leimert like red-eyed Hobbits in a stoner remake of *The Lord of the Rings*. Pulling up to Leimert Park felt like stepping onto a battlefield: a hundred people scattered across the intersection, cyphers erupting like fires in the night. A mélange of beats came from every corner—car stereos, boomboxes, and people beatboxing. Though B-boys and graffiti artists were milling around, it was the place for MCs to shine. Rappers hopped from cypher to cypher like Dr. Strange portals. The demographic was nothing like my local school cypher.

The breakdown was about 80 percent Black and 20 percent Latino, all men. The few Asian Americans I saw that night were filming and taking photos.

Much more interesting than the racial makeup was the cast of characters within this eclectic scene: Black anime nerds and punk-rock types mixed with Crips and Bloods, incense guys, and spaced-out druggies with names like Riddlore, Acid Reign, Teradacto, Psychosiz, and Open Mike Eagle. Forget Area 51, this was a mutant academy: Xavier's School for Gifted Young MCs. The rap styles were similarly diverse, from head-wrapped, neo-soul conscious rappers to flag-wearing gangbangers to unorthodox, abstract MCs who defied categorization. Myka 9 used his voice and words like Coltrane jamming on his saxophone. Rifleman, as his moniker suggests, shot off a hundred words per minute like a machine gun. Busdriver did avant-garde indie rock in freestyle-rap form, painting multisyllabic words in the air with his fingers. It was a total mindfuck of styles in all directions.

My musical influences up to that point were what played on the radio, plus a few underground New York rappers with a more traditional, straightforward delivery and cadence. And my exposure to Black people had largely been limited to TV and movie stereotypes. Project Blowed was like the hip-hop I grew up on . . . on acid. But if this was new territory, it was where I was supposed to be.

A Cypher Incomplete

Project Blowed consisted of two distinct areas: outside the KAOS building, where rappers scattered around the corner and into the adjacent park to form on-the-fly cyphers; and inside the building, which functioned more like a traditional open mic with a sign-up sheet for rappers to perform original songs. Since I hadn't recorded any music before my first visit to Blowed, I remained outside to freestyle—and honestly, that was the place to be. Inside, you could get acknowledged as a good songwriter and stage performer, but outside, you could gain respect as a freestyler and battle rapper. It was the difference between the NBA and AND1 streetball. I've always been a street kid at heart, so I naturally gravitated to the cyphers.

At Blowed, freestyling was respected above all else. Proficiency at off-the-dome rapping was how legends were made, and those who excelled built on their Blowed reputations to conquer other battlegrounds. For example, a regular named Otherwize famously defeated Eminem at the 1997 Rap Olympics. At the 1999 Scribble Jam, the Super Bowl of battle rap, P.E.A.C.E. made it all the way to the finals. I immediately knew that I wanted to be a part of this lineage of legends. I wanted to be a Blowedian.

To achieve that title, I first had to actually find the courage to join a cypher. That first night, witnessing the intimidating throngs of rappers circling outside, my mind was blowed—pun intended. Clouds of blunt smoke permeated the block and tickled my nostrils; the Swisher Sweets cigar guts littering the ground looked like little anthills. From a young stoner's perspective, this was heaven on Earth.

There were no friendly angels out here, though. As I made my way around the cyphers, my every move felt scrutinized. The regulars either ignored you or stared you down, silently daring you to prove yourself. No one was gonna welcome or make space for you. The vibe was starkly different from my school cafeteria, where I walked around like I had three-hundred-pound balls and spit rhymes without hesitation. In Leimert Park, I was a timid little freshman trying to cut a line of upperclassmen. An established hierarchy existed there, and everyone knew who the top dogs were. The OGs had the right of way because they'd been around for years and paid their dues.

James, who was a fan of my freestyles at school, started gassing me up and pressuring me to hop in a cypher.

Robbie nudged me in the back. "Get in there, foo!"

I told them both to chill while I checked the temperature and surveyed the lay of the land. Like day one in jail, I had to learn the proper etiquette before making my first move. As I passed one cypher, I heard some of the most intricate multisyllabic rhymes I'd ever heard, followed by ecstatic *damns* and *whoos* from the crowd after each bar. When I finally made it to the front, I saw the rapper commanding all the attention: Nocando—yes, like the chorus from the Hall & Oates song—an eighteen-year-old Black kid in a camo shirt and tight Dickies. He was so quick-witted that I doubted his rhymes were coming from the top of his head until he instantly ripped a comeback at another rapper who tried to clown him about his tight pants. I felt like a typewriter staring at an iMac.

As I was listening to Nocando rap, others hopped in the cypher, and soon a new MC took over. In this environment, nobody passed the mic. You had to jump in and take it, interrupting whoever was rapping to get your bars in, which was often how battles kicked off. This was not the friendly and orderly "You go, I go" dynamic in the cafeteria.

Thirty minutes passed, then an hour. Rapper after rapper hopped in and traded freestyles, like timing a double-Dutch entrance. Two hours passed, and I still couldn't find the nerve to clear my throat and speak up. Every time I thought there was an opening, I froze. Thursday night soon turned into Friday morning.

At about one a.m., with the crowd thinning, James said, "Yo, I gotta go, it's getting late."

I shrugged and agreed. As we trudged back to the Civic, an immense disappointment settled in. Seeing Blowed in person showed me a humbling new reality. My ego was deflated; I had failed. Even my friends were disheartened by my cold feet. Usually, we'd leave a house party after I rapped for hours, and they'd crowd around me adoringly—their trophy rapper, the pride and joy of the crew. Tonight, I was exposed as an absolute nobody.

In the backseat of the Civic on the way back to Ktown, staring at the L.A. skyline, I replayed the night's events in my head. My inner monologue gnawed at me.

Fuck, I should've hopped in. You're such a coward.

Damn, those fools were hella good.

I felt like Kirsten Dunst in *Bring It On* when she realizes she and her team are frauds compared to the East Compton Clovers. I was down—but far from defeated. I vowed to come back week after week to prove that I belonged at Blowed. For now, it was back to the drawing board.

Practice Makes Wordsmiths

I couldn't sleep that night thinking about what I'd experienced. It wasn't just the leftover adrenaline from walking through a gauntlet of freestyle killers, but also my overwhelming ambition to reach their level. The next day at school was even worse; all I could think about was Blowed. I watched the clock tick by, feeling like I was wasting time when I could be getting better at freestyling. I'd finally found an institution I respected and wanted to invest my time in. Fuck a diploma, I was gonna be a Blowedian.

My high school cafeteria, my old stomping ground, now felt like a preschool sandbox. To hang with the pros, I'd have to take rapping more seriously. Never one for studying, I suddenly turned into a research fiend. I used Napster to download music from Project Blowed artists, looking up battles and freestyles from the names I'd overheard that night. I was like an obsessed hacker going down a rabbit hole, poring over albums like Freestyle Fellowship's *To Whom It May Concern . . .* and *Innercity Griots,* as well as the original 1995 Project Blowed compilation.

I wasn't only studying the craft, I was practicing it too. I stepped up the number of hours spent freestyling per day, like my own personal rap Kumon. I was behind and needed to catch up. The rappers at Blowed looked like Olympic athletes: eyes wide open, veins bulging out of their necks, words piercing the air like daggers. I needed to get into game shape.

Around this time, I landed on my rap name. One afternoon, my friends and I got stoned and flipped through a dictionary for ideas, picking out random words that sounded cool. In the *D* section, I stumbled on *dumbfounded.* It sounded funny and fit my personality as the class clown. The definition sealed it: "speechless with amazement; astonished or showing astonishment." Perfect. My raps did leave people dumbfounded. To make it more unique and searchable, I added the *a* at the end to turn it into a double entendre: Dumb. Found. Dead. Dumbfoundead. My friends loved the name, so I ran with it.

I started to wake up thinking of rhymes. My toothbrush would be in one hand as I wrote rhymes in the air with the other:

Colgate, Cobain, road rage, sorbet, foreplay

On the bus to school:
Metro, West Coast, Velcro, escrow

In the Marshall High parking lot:
Marlboro Light, arson fire, dark as night

The rhymes didn't have to be perfect or make sense. Practicing them felt like training for a fight. My brain was the gym, and every word became my sparring partner. I clocked reps online through keystyling, a nerdy version of freestyling that was popular on message boards like AZNRaps.com and rapmusic.com. Instead of rapping a verse out loud, I'd type it into a post to "battle" other posters. That's where I first learned of Danny Chung, aka Decipher, from Philadelphia, and Rick Lee, aka Lyricks, out of Virginia—two of my closest friends to this day, who now both write for K-pop superstars. Keystyling was a fun cure for boredom, but I still thought my battle stripes were untouchable. I'd post shit like, "You know where to find me! On the corner of 43rd and Leimert every Thursday night!" The truth was, the majority of AZNRaps posters never rhymed on the block. Theirs wasn't a street corner, but a message board. But because they were Internet savvy, they were also uploading their recorded music, which made me realize they had a head start.

My mom and sister would often catch me drifting off while I mentally composed multisyllabic rhyme schemes, like Russell Crowe in *A Beautiful Mind*. My mom always suspected I was high—and OK, I was—but I was more addicted to rhyming than weed. The albums

I studied opened up my mind like I'd taken the *Limitless* pill. I was listening to artists who weren't confined by rules, so I unknowingly broke them before I even learned them. Ultimately, it was a gift and a curse, but learning as I go has always been my style—I've literally freestyled my entire life. I never had structure growing up, so why would my rap style?

Damn, Jackie Chan Can Spit!

As I put in the requisite hours of study and practice, my confidence grew. Still, it wasn't until my fourth time at Blowed that I felt ready to join the fray. That night, I weaved through the crowd and rushed to the nearest cypher. Like jumping into the cold ocean, I needed to run in headfirst rather than take it slow and possibly chicken out. As I gathered my composure, I found an opening and took a deep breath. I managed to rap about eight bars before someone cut me off and took over. OK, so it wasn't exactly the Beatles on *The Ed Sullivan Show*. I only heard crickets from the stone-faced crowd, who didn't appreciate how much I'd prepared for this very moment. But I was still proud of myself. The crippling fear subsided. I could hang. A huge grin stayed plastered on my face all night. However, popping my Blowed cherry isn't my fondest memory of those early days. While I'd conquered the first obstacle—muscling into a cypher to spit a freestyle—to really cement my rep at Blowed meant I had to battle.

I grew up watching Jackie Chan movies and admired the way his characters avoided confrontation until they were left with no choice but to react. He'd be minding his own business when an enemy would start attacking him. Jackie would wave his hands in protest and exclaim in a thick Chinese accent, "I don't want no trouble!" Then, pushed to the edge, he'd be forced to fight back and, inevitably, humiliate his attacker incorporating his trademark comedic fighting style. I reacted the same way the first time I was hit with a stray, which was a random diss from somebody in a cypher. I didn't want to hurt anybody, but now I had to.

The following week at Blowed, I was standing in a cypher when someone suddenly pointed at me and hit me with a quick stray: *The weed got my eyes chinky like this dude.* A smattering of laughter from onlookers followed.

Seizing the moment, I stepped in to defend myself. *Yeah, my eyes slanted, but in Asia we clown bug eyes like yours that are gigantic.* The crowd went crazy. No, it wasn't the cleverest punchline, but the surprising speed of the comeback got the cypher buzzing.

Out of nowhere, someone shouted, "*Damn*, Jackie Chan can spit!"

I was minding my business, got attacked, fought back, and won. That comment replayed in my head for the rest of the year. Except, I hit the middle beat harder: "Damn, Jackie Chan *can* spit." It wasn't exactly a coronation, but a victory nonetheless. The validation was intoxicating—funny how my most memorable compliment was wrapped in a stereotypical diss. I felt I belonged there. Battling became my new religion, and I was now a true believer. Thursday night at Blowed became my Sunday service.

Nocando told me that to become a Blowedian, you needed three main qualities. One, you had to treat Blowed like church and attend regularly, ideally every week. *Check.* Two, you had to be accepted by the Blowed regulars. That didn't mean assimilating to fit in. In fact, the weirder and more original you sounded, the better. It meant you had to respect the community and what it stood for. *Check.* And three, you had to stand out. This meant opening up, letting go, and losing yourself in the magical, Earth-leaving rush of fearless creation. Those were the moments that Blowed veterans noticed, like, "Oh, you're one of us." Week by week, I became further engulfed in the scene. Before long, it was I in the center of the circle, wowing everybody with my rhymes. *Check.*

When class let out on Thursdays, I would count down the minutes until James scooped me up in his mom's Civic and drove us to South Central. If he wasn't able to go, I had to find another way to travel the five miles from Ktown to Leimert Park. Occasionally, I took the MTA bus; other times, a Razor scooter. Sometimes, I even ran back home to make sure no gangbanger attacked me in the early hours past midnight. Blowed itself was considered neutral ground, even if you were gang-affiliated; but the threat of violence was never far. Once, I remember a guy freestyling, and a gun fell down his pant leg. We all heard the *click-clack* as it skipped across the concrete. Meanwhile, the cypher kept going like nothing happened. Despite the danger, the risk was well worth it. Whatever strife I faced at home became bearable once I found Blowed. My family life was still coming apart at the seams, but at least I had an outlet where I could shine.

Signing Up Is Half the Battle

I'd overcome my hesitation to perform outside the building at Project Blowed, but another world existed inside. After about a year of freestyling outside, I finally mustered up the courage to try my luck inside. Within the walls of 4343 Leimert Boulevard, rappers signed up to perform their own songs in front of an audience. The sign-up sheet read: "$2 if You Sign This List & Rhyme, $4 If You Don't O.K.?" Below it was "da muthaf**ckin rulz" as laid out by Ben, the owner.

You Are Now About To Enter

project blowed

READ THIS FIRST!!!!!

- ✓ NO **SMOKING** OR **DRINKING ALCOHOL** IN HERE! The owner has "requested" that this be a no-alcohol, no smoking business. Fa' sho'.
- ✓ THERE IS OPEN MIKE AT THE *BEGINNING* AND AT THE *END*. NO ONE WHO IS NOT CALLED FROM THE LIST BY THE HOST CAN GET ON STAGE *AT ANY OTHER TIME*! REMEMBER THAT!
- ✓ This is a Hip Hop Educational Seminar, where styles are shown so many can learn and grow. *DO NOT BITE STYLES*, BECAUSE YOU LEARN NOTHING! **DO NOT GET VIOLENT**, BECAUSE THIS IS A BLACK-OWNED, BLACK-OPERATED BUSINESS THAT CAN'T AFFORD TO HEAR THAT! **Take that stuff to WestWood**.
- ✓ Project Blowed is presented for the love of hip hop entirely by Black people. However, it **can't** get done if everybody's bills don't get paid, so we charge the "participants" TWO DOLLARS to practice their styles, and we charge FOUR DOLLARS to people who want to watch education at work. This pays for using the building, the sound, and keeping it going on - also known as THE CAUSE of keeping hip hop underground.

project blowed

Brought to you by ...
A-TEAM
RODUCTIONS
KAOS
Network
and
Afterlife

won	1	
too	2	
tree	3	
fo'	4	
fahve	5	
sicks	6	
seben	7	
eiht	8	
(tell?) nahne	9	
tin	10	
eleben	11	
won-too	12	
won-tree	13	
fo'-teen	14	
fit'-teen	15	
won-sez	16	
seben-teen	17	
won-eiht	18	
won-9	19	
a dub	20	

Da Cost Uv Da Cause

$2 if You Sign This List & Rhyme

$4 If You Don't

O.K.?

da mutha f**ckin' rulz ↓

Upon entering the space, I saw a glass display case filled with mixtapes, patches, and merch from Blowed alumni such as the Freestyle Fellowship. Graffiti and African tribal art pieces covered the walls. The thick smell of incense permeated the air. In the main room, a crowd gathered before a small stage with a DJ and a host. The vibe was communal yet unforgiving, like an underground rap version of *Showtime at the Apollo*. If the Blowed audience wasn't feeling you, they'd start chanting, "Please pass the mic, please pass the mic," while you were still performing. (At least they said "please.") The house DJ would abruptly stop the beat mid-performance, like someone bumped the turntables at a house party. This brutal, humbling feedback showed you in real time the audience's appetite for your performance. After being rudely dismissed, some rappers threw the mic down and got angry at the crowd, like, "Fuck you, I don't care what any of y'all think. This shit hard!" Others merely slumped their shoulders in disappointment before slinking off stage. If you got the hook, you had two choices: go home and never return, or keep coming back until you stop getting passed. Tough love, but I was used to that already.

It took some stones for me to put my name on that sign-up sheet, but that was only half the battle. I had understood this from an early age. Without fail, I signed myself up for all types of performances—because the moment you sign up, you have to go through with it. There's no turning back. In third grade, I volunteered for the school play and landed the role of the Tin Man in our rendition of *The Wiz*. (I can still sing "Ease on Down the Road" by heart.) At age eleven, I auditioned at a local mall, which led to a role in a commercial. In my late teens, I did spoken-word and stand-up comedy open mics before I had any idea how to do either. When I started going to L.A.

freestyle battles, I performed in competitions where two random names would be called on stage to battle each other. When you sign up for something, they're gonna call your name. And when they do, you'd better be ready.

Was I nervous the first time I registered to perform at Project Blowed? Or for that matter, anything else I impulsively signed up for over the years? The answer is: Yes, always. But the anxiety pales in comparison to the roller coaster of adrenaline that hits my bloodstream when I hear my name. I have no qualms about forcing myself into uncomfortable situations, especially if someone tells me I can't do it. Nothing fuels me more than doubt. I still keep a running list of quotes from people in my past who've doubted me:

- Stacey Ahn, second grade: "You'll never be famous!"
- Kent C., at a rap show in 2006: "He's a good *underground* rapper, but he'll never go mainstream."
- Malek3259, in the comments of a 2014 YouTube video: "People only fuck with Dumb because he's Asian."
- Bobby Lee, on my podcast in 2022: "You'll never become an action star." (Keep doubting, Bobby. I'm well on my way.)

So, having broken the ice at Blowed, I signed up to perform inside. Using FruityLoops, I'd produced the song I was going to perform. Maybe my third-grade performance in *The Wiz* was still on my mind, because I named the track "The Wizard of L.A." and wrote lyrics about Los Angeles using *The Wizard of Oz* references.

My nerves jangled as I stood inside the darkened room, awaiting my turn on the mic. I watched a procession of MCs step on stage and try their luck, the majority of them getting jeered off.

"Aight, yo, next on the list: Dumb . . . founder? Dumbfoundead?"

My friends nudged me, shouting words of encouragement—"You got this!" "Kill it!"—as I stepped into the spotlight.

The DJ dropped the beat. I grabbed the mic, cleared my throat, and began.

Around here, we like to call them pigs
The dealer down the street, his alias is "Wiz"

I tried to ignore the muffled groan I heard from the middle of the crowd.

Emerald City ain't really where he lives
It's actually a no-bedroom, shitty-ass crib

I noticed the audience moving a little bit. Were they feeling it? Or just restless and bored?

Walk over with me to the City of Angels
Where the way we live is dependent on a payroll

I saw a pair of raised arms in the audience, moving in sync with the beat. A small victory.

But then, a disquieting rumble rose from the back. Like a wave, it rolled through the thicket and toward the stage.

"Please . . ."

I'm now into my second verse.

". . . pass . . ."

It can't be.

". . . the MIC!"

So yeah, I got "pass the mic"-ed off stage. It was my first time bombing in front of an audience, and truthfully, I wasn't performance ready. I signaled to the homies, and we immediately left the venue.

"I don't want to talk about it," I muttered as they tried to critique what I could've done better. My mic control was sloppy. It was the wrong song choice. I didn't have enough confidence to move the crowd.

"Maybe you should stick to the cyphers," said James.

Maybe *what*? Remember what I said about people doubting me?

Performing inside was different from battling outside—it demanded polish and presence, not just quick wit. But as with any of my failures, persistence was everything. Within months, I signed up again to rap inside Project Blowed. And once again, I performed "The Wizard of L.A." This time, I made it through the entire song and even got some cheers. Don't believe me? Search "Dumbfoundead @ Project Blowed" on YouTube.

After a year at Blowed, I still hadn't considered making rap a career. I was broke as hell but rich with community, a stray cat who finally found a place and a family to call home. There was something special about Blowed, culturally and spiritually. Different crews coexisted there, bearing names like 2000 Crows, Customer Service, and my clique, Swim Team. We even had a logo with a ship's anchor and a slogan below it that read "Holdin' Shit Down." Despite our differences, we were collective-minded and tenacious. For me, freestyling and battling had evolved from an escape to a way forward—toward a sanctuary and a new identity. I had become Dumbfoundead, standing toe-to-toe with the best.

CHAPTER FOUR

RAP HEROES

Before we proceed, I feel like I haven't talked about rap enough, or at least, who my influences were. Rap fans are notorious for trotting out their top five rappers of all time—Chris Rock even premised an entire movie off the idea—and the names you hear, give or take an obscure name or two, are usually the same. If you asked me for my top five—and to be honest, I hate the question—you'd probably be unsurprised to hear names like 2Pac, Ice Cube, Redman, and Biggie. As a teenage rap fan in the early aughts, I consumed everything from West Coast gangster rap to East Coast boom bap to Southern shit from Cash Money, Dungeon Family, and No Limit.

However, the list I've compiled here is a little different. It's less about fandom and more about who I wanted to be as an MC. Each of these figures represents a different kind of opponent in the larger battle to define myself as a rapper—an idol to emulate, a sensei to be inspired by, a mentor to guide me, and a rival to challenge.

So, it's not even a top five; it's a top four. Call it my Mount Rushmore. See, even that rhymed.

Eminem (The Idol)

On that fateful night in 2001, when I finally built up the courage to enter a Project Blowed cypher, I was a wild card in a deck of Black and Brown faces. I could feel the weight of the crowd's curiosity about how I would sound or what I would say. And then, I bore down and mustered the courage to rap. That was my Eminem moment.

In his rap battles, both in the film *8 Mile* and in real life, Em played up the shock value of his whiteness. His opponents would get visibly frustrated at how the crowd would lose their minds over Em's wordplay—not only because it was clever, but also because it was so unusual to see a white guy snapping on the mic. I've long said that being Asian or white in rap is both a gift and a curse.

Eminem being an outlier in an all-Black space was only part of the reason I related to him so much. Purely based on his rhyming ability and creativity, Em was a huge influence on my style. Years before "My Name Is" and *8 Mile* made him a household name, Eminem was already famous to me and other rabid fans of the underground battle circuit. But unlike the end of the movie, Em didn't always emerge victorious. In the mid- to late 1990s, there were nationwide freestyle battle competitions like Scribble Jam and the Rap Olympics, where the best of the best competed. Though he was an incredible freestyler, Eminem took back-to-back Ls in 1997. First, he lost to the legend J.U.I.C.E. at Scribble Jam in Cincinnati; then he lost to Project Blowed alum Otherwize at the Rap Olympics in L.A. That latter battle has become the stuff of lore because no video or audio of it has ever been seen or heard. Shortly after the event, Dr.

Dre signed the white rapper from Detroit to his Aftermath Records, and Em boarded a rocket ship to stardom. Some believe that Dre bought and buried the Rap Olympics footage because he didn't want anyone to see his prized prospect lose.

If that Otherwize–Eminem audio exists, trust me, I would've found it. During the Napster era—roughly between the years of 1999 and 2001—I religiously downloaded recordings of all sorts of battles and radio freestyles from Eminem as well as rappers like Royce da 5'9", Supernatural, Eyedea, Slug, Freeway, Cassidy, Canibus, and Big L. That was the era when many MCs still legitimately freestyled off the top, sometimes weaving in words that were thrown at them on the spot. In subsequent years, rap battles became less about improv and more about carefully researched premeds, or lines thought of beforehand, i.e., premeditated. But true freestyle rapping was what I loved the most—it wasn't just part of hip-hop, but its own art form where people could create something brilliant and funny in real time. I lived and breathed those pirated freestyles, running them back over and over again.

Beyond his whiteness, Eminem clearly stood out. In his early radio freestyles—which, to be clear, were often prewritten raps—you'd hear the hosts on the side laughing at how over-the-top his rhymes were.

Drivin' a rusty scalpel in through the top of your scalp
And pullin' your Adam's apple out through your mouth
Better call the fire department, I've hired an arsonist
To set fire to carpet, and burn up your entire apartment

To the ears of an aspiring teenage rapper, Em's cartoonishly violent lyrics were like rap anime: eyeballs popping out, heads exploding, severed limbs flailing. His unfiltered streams of thought inspired me to say unhinged things in my rhymes too. But it wasn't just the crudeness that appealed to me. I was a true rhyme nerd, and Em was an absolute technician. The multisyllabic wordplay was original, and so was the dexterity of his enunciation—he bent words into origami shapes to match the beat. Truthfully, Eminem was a nerd too—or at least an antisocial loser. Which meant that he had fewer limitations as an artist than what was prescribed by the machismo rap blueprint that we all grew up with. Instead of talking about how bitches were all on his nuts, he almost went full incel. Yeah, his lyrics were equally problematic in their own way, but for me they were refreshing. I was a teenager holding up size 36 Phat Farm jeans for eight hours a day, just to look cool. It was exhausting.

Em taught me to relax a little bit because he was making a career doing what I wanted to do and had all kinds of fucked-up issues. He sounded like a dude who knew what it felt like to get bullied, and I'd been there too. Yet he rhymed with the confidence of someone who *was* the bully. Rapping turned him into a superhero—or maybe a supervillain—and I felt the same way. He was also a role model in another way because he broke the stigma of battle rappers being unable to translate their prowess into equally good recorded music.

Eventually, as I became more known as a rapper, a lot of people compared me to Eminem. I used to hate hearing it because it was such a hard thing to live up to. Some rando would come up to me and say, "You're gonna do this, bro, you're the Asian Eminem!" Oh, you mean the best-selling rapper of all time?

Of course, I'm flattered to even be mentioned in the same paragraph as Em. After all, we both got our start in battle rap as marginalized underdogs. We both starred in films about the scene, even if mine—2017's *Bodied*, which Eminem executive-produced—didn't come close to an Oscar. We overenunciate our words with nasal deliveries. We subvert racial stereotypes and use humor as a signature weapon. But . . . I've always loved my mom.

(RIP Debbie Mathers.)

Jin (The Sensei)

The final battle in *8 Mile* delivered an unforgettable lesson: Beat your opponent to the punch. As Sun Tzu preached in *The Art of War*, knowing both your enemy and yourself is the key to victory. In the film, B-Rabbit anticipates that Papa Doc is going to attack him about his white-trash upbringing. So, he preemptively uses those disses against himself—*I am white, I am a fucking bum / I do live in a trailer with my mom*—effectively rendering them useless. B-Rabbit knew his enemy would try to exploit his weaknesses, and he was prepared.

And so was Jin. If the pioneering Mountain Brothers from Philly were the Cold Crush Brothers of Asian American rappers, then Jin was our LL Cool J—a charismatic, mainstream star. The son of Hong Kong immigrants, he grew up in Miami and moved to NYC when he was nineteen to pursue his rap dreams. When he unexpectedly broke through, he shifted the tectonic plates, clearing the way for me and other Asian American rappers who followed.

In the early 2000s, as rap battles became slightly more mainstream, one of the most prominent stages was on BET's *106 & Park* in a weekly segment called "Freestyle Friday." Two MCs squared off, with each given thirty seconds to spit a battle verse over a beat; a panel of celebrity judges declared the winner. Whoever won on a given Friday would return the following week to face a new challenger. When the segment premiered, I remember thinking, *I can't wait to be the first Asian rapper on Freestyle Friday!* But damn it, along came Jin—beating me to the punch.

Beginning in February 2002, Jin dominated Freestyle Friday for seven straight weeks, defeating a new opponent each time. It was the rap equivalent of Jeremy Lin's "Linsanity" run—call it Jinsanity. An Asian rapper fearlessly defeating all competitors under a nationally televised spotlight was unheard of. His streak earned him a spot in the Freestyle Friday Hall of Fame and a record deal with Ruff Ryders Entertainment. Watching Jin dominate on a huge stage didn't just make me proud—it made me hungry. If he could do it, maybe I could too.

It wasn't just *what* Jin did, but *how* he did it: by absorbing bad Asian joke after bad Asian joke and Uno-reversing that energy to shut down his adversaries.

My pants are new, my sweater is new
Don't be mad a Chinese kid dressed better than you!

Ask your girl, I was doin' somethin' at her house
Matter fact, she had my egg roll and my dumplings in her mouth!

You wanna say I'm Chinese, sonny? Here's a reminder
Check your Timbs, they probably say "Made in China!"

That last "Check your Timbs" snap became an iconic line and exemplifies why Jin went undefeated. It's race-based but doesn't feel hacky; it's simple, effective, and rooted in reality.

For obvious reasons, Jin became a huge inspiration for me. That February, as he began his run, I was a high school freshman who had just caught the battle bug at Project Blowed. Pretty soon, I was racing home from school every Friday afternoon to catch Jin's nationally televised battles on BET. Naturally, I was rooting for him because he was Asian, even if he wasn't necessarily relatable from a rhyming perspective. Our styles were totally different. Jin was very much an East Coast MC in cadence, slang, and delivery. Appearance, too: Jin's razor-sharp skin fade was straight New York. But it didn't matter. I was just excited to see an Asian kid destroy his opposition, especially by using the comedic style of freestyle roasting that I also favored.

What also drew me in was the fact that Jin didn't resort to shock factor or some clichéd shtick to win. He didn't come out wielding a samurai sword or donning a straw hat. There was no misdirection gimmick at play. Instead, he looked like someone fully immersed in early-aughts hip-hop culture, rocking full Enyce sweat suits and bucket hats. Jin later told me that for the first six weeks of Freestyle Friday, he wore the only six outfits he brought with him to NYC from Miami after his family had to suddenly relocate. For the final week, he wore a free outfit given to him by the brand Akademiks—which, Asian, Akademiks . . . the sponsorship makes sense.

Jin didn't need to lean into Asian stereotypes to authentically represent as one. There were a few prominent Asians in the rap game—Fresh Kid Ice from 2 Live Crew, apl.de.ap from Black Eyed Peas, Southstar from Smilez & Southstar, and Far East Movement, for example—but those guys were part of groups. There were no mainstream Asian American solo artists. It hit differently to see Jin rep his heritage, by himself, at the forefront. He even broke out into Cantonese at the end of one battle—on Black Entertainment Television.

Jin is forever in the history books. If someone who knows nothing about rap meets me and finds out I'm a rapper, it's not long before they'll say, "Do you remember that one Asian dude from Freestyle Friday?" Yes, I do. And I still run back those Freestyle Friday battles on YouTube several times a year as a refresher.

The postscript to Jin's story: After his Freestyle Friday buzz, it took almost two years until the release of his first single—unsubtly titled "Learn Chinese"—and subsequent debut album, *The Rest Is History,* which came out in 2004. (In between, he played the mechanic Jimmy in the 2003 movie *2 Fast 2 Furious.*) Jin continued to participate in battles but struggled to keep pace when the era of premed raps overtook off-the-top freestyles, which were his specialty. Perhaps his lowest point came when he faced the New Jersey rapper Serius Jones in a 2005 Fight Klub battle televised on MTV2. Jones hit Jin with the immortal line: *Ain't it two billion people in China? / You can't even go platinum over there!* Ouch.

But since then, Jin actually *did* find success as an entertainer in Hong Kong, as both a musician and an actor. These days, he's a married father of two, splitting time between the States and China. A devout Christian, Jin's still nice with the freestyles—and literally the nicest person you could ever meet. Maybe even too nice to battle—unless it's one of those "compliment" battles that have picked up steam in recent years.

If Eminem taught me to embrace my inner chaos, Jin showed me how to turn that chaos into cultural pride.

Nocando (The Mentor)

I've been hit with so many battle lines in my life that remembering them all would be impossible. But one immediately comes to mind: *I'll beat your ass like a Korean dad when you bring home a B in math.* It came from the mouth of my Project Blowed friend—and occasional foe—Nocando.

Nocando represented the next generation of Blowedians after legends like Freestyle Fellowship. Those guys were the forefathers who innovated the craft of freestyle and battling, and people like Nocando carried the torch. When I first got into the scene, I looked up to him, and he took me on as a protégé. To me, he's not just the best L.A. freestyler and battler of his generation, but also a mentor who shaped my approach to the art.

Nocando is three years older than me. When we first met, he was eighteen and already expecting his first kid. While I was just a teenage rookie learning how to battle for sport, this motherfucker was out here battling for diaper money. He felt like my Black older brother, even in the way he presented himself: a slightly nerdy-looking skinny kid rocking schmedium skater shirts, tight Dickies, dirty Chucks, and trucker hats. He was a self-proclaimed hippie and didn't look like anybody else in South Central at the time—he looked more like he was in a hardcore band than a rapper. Maybe he saw me—also a slightly nerdy-looking skinny kid in a schmedium shirt and dirty Chucks—and felt immediate kinship. Gangsta battle rappers who weren't familiar with Nocando would try to battle him because they judged him on his appearance—only to be utterly destroyed when he unleashed his bars. In fact, fending off the doubters is probably why Nocan became so adept at battling. He was so nasty with his rhyme schemes that he earned everybody's respect.

As I studied the freestyle space more, I saw a couple of distinct categories of rappers: the overly aggressive types who leaned toward gangster personas and the multisyllabic wizards who embraced their nerddom. What made Nocan stand out was his ability to bridge those two worlds. He took the intricate rhymes favored by nerdy white kids in the freestyle space and added a sharp edge and undeniable swag, delivering impossibly prolific punchlines, impossibly fast.

You try to act sick, like you're Grind Time's Hannibal Lecter
But on the inside you're softer than a handful of feathers
To beat you, I don't have to be tactical ever
I'll be practical; pressure
You're so much of a bitch that if you ran away from home you'd come home pregnant from the animal shelter

I later learned that Nocando didn't even listen to rap growing up in L.A.—he was a grunge, KROQ kid. He got expelled from high school in ninth grade and sent up north to Fairfield to live with his father. Tragically, that same year, his dad passed away, and Nocan came back to L.A. Like me, he found a creative outlet in rap and a sanctuary in Project Blowed. He was freestyling on an MTA bus one day in 1999 when he encountered a dreadlocked old head who was making beats on a little Roland SP-404 portable sampler. The dreadhead saw Nocan rapping and said, "You should check out this spot on Leimert called Freestyle Fellowship," referring to Project Blowed by the name of its most famous alumni. Nocan liked the name, thinking it sounded like a church of rap, so he showed up. Immediately, he was hooked by the competition and the dopamine rush of performing there. Before long, he was a regular.

I met Nocando at Blowed, where I—and everyone else—viewed him as the leader of the new school. His flow, his punchlines, even his appearance—it all clicked for me and influenced my still-developing style. The first time I saw him hold court in a cypher, I remember thinking, *I wouldn't mind sounding like this dude.* Nocan's use of humor was especially notable to me. For unimposing guys like him and me, it was a much more effective battle tactic than "I'm gonna fuck you up." Because nobody would believe that, including myself. Nocan led a crew called Customer Service, who at the time were the youngest on the scene—until my crew, Swim Team, came along as the best new-school dudes. We'd continue to cross paths at various L.A. hip-hop battles. The same names usually advanced to the finals: me, Dizaster, Destruct, and Nocando. But Nocan was on another level—I've never beaten him in a final. Yes, he beat my ass like a Korean dad when I brought home a B in math. (Just with words, not a shoehorn.)

In 2007, Nocando won the crown jewel of battle rap, Scribble Jam, bringing the trophy back to L.A. We were all stoked, because in a way it felt like a win for all of Blowed. Later, Nocando ditched his name and now goes by All City Jimmy. The children he once supported through his art are grown now, and one's even in college.

While Jin inspired me to see what was possible for Asian rappers on a national stage, Nocando grounded me in the art of freestyle and helped me sharpen my craft.

Lyricks (The Rival)

By the time I was nineteen, I felt like I was the best Asian American rapper alive—and if not the best of all Asians, at the very least, the best among Koreans. (And at the very, very least, the best in Koreatown.) I had cut my teeth in the pressure cooker every Thursday night at Project Blowed. When I was back in Ktown rapping with my peers, nobody could touch me.

In the summer of 2007, I was onstage in a basketball gym at Lafayette Park, trading freestyles with Koreatown locals. There was an informal open mic for Asian rappers held there called Jeet Kune Flow, a play on Bruce Lee's martial art, Jeet Kune Do. In that circle, everyone acknowledged me as the king of the court.

We were in a cypher trading verses, when all of a sudden, the gym door swung open, its slam reverberating across the room. In walked an unmistakably Korean rapper, accompanied by an older Korean guy who seemed to be his manager. The rapper looked almost like a college athlete, down to the square-jawed face, fit physique, and matching sweat suit. The cypher paused, every head turning toward the entrance as the sound of their footsteps echoed ominously across the parquet floor: *doom . . . doom . . . DOOM*. It was like a scene out of *The Karate Kid*: Johnny Lawrence strutting into the dojo with his Cobra Kai sensei John Kreese. I sized him up with arrogant skepticism.

The rapper introduced himself as Lyricks—a backward flip of his government name, Rick Lee. We dapped each other up and freestyling resumed. It soon became clear to the rest of the group that he was . . . well, shit, he was pretty nice and could really rap. Like, damn, this dude was going off.

One by one, the others ran out of gas, stepping back until it was just Lyricks and me, trading lines like boxers in the final round of an unofficial bout. We went on for hours, trying to one-up each other with clever lines. His delivery was precise, and his freestyle was impressive. The mutual respect was earned. Whenever I cypher with somebody new, I can quickly discern whether that person has got skills—and if they do, whether or not we have enough in common to become friends. Suffice it to say, Lyricks and I became close. Of course, as soon as he left the gym, my friends started egging me on to see him as a rival: "Oh, Dumb, he kind of got you."

In the age before social media, I didn't even realize that Lyricks was already making a name as one of the top Asian rappers. Originally from Virginia, he had recently moved to L.A. to further his career. I wouldn't have guessed it from our first cypher, but Lyricks identified as a Christian rapper—a persona I instinctively thought was corny. But being a Christian rapper brought him a lot of cachet in the Asian community. Most Korean American kids were associated with the church, and here was one of their own, spitting deep-cutting lyrics on emotional songs about Christianity and faith.

We're taught that you're intentional, God, but I'm nervous
Maybe it's my lack of faith, but I'm here questioning the purpose
I feel defeated but still believe that you're perfect
So, like Job, instead of scorning you I'm just choosing to worship

What Korean parent wouldn't want their kids to listen to that? I know my mom would bump that in the whip.

I couldn't deny that Lyricks was great on the mic. My rapping style was profane, quick-witted, and freewheeling, and I looked like a little rascal from the streets. Lyricks rapped in a traditional, boom-bap, straightforward MC style, and he had the visuals of the popular jock in high school. I made a song called "Blue Ball Blues"; he made one called "Blessed Be His Name."

Inevitably, a healthy competition developed. We were similar in certain ways: both aspiring Korean American MCs with younger sisters. I admit that even though I befriended Lyricks, I felt a little threatened by him, because every Korean in the church circuit seemed to be rooting for him. In many ways, he was the classic good Korean kid: His hardworking parents ran a dry-cleaning business in Virginia while their morally upright son journeyed on church missions to Uganda to spread God's word. Lyricks was so much easier for the Korean community to love than I was, the wisecracking stoner from a broken home. I actually had to thank God that he wanted to do Christian rap, since that was a whole separate world.

However, our worlds collided that same year we met, at the 2007 edition of Kollaboration, a talent showcase started by my comedian friend Paul "PK" Kim for Asian performers. Soon-to-be stars like Jo Koy got their start there. Part of that evening's show was a rap battle; both Lyricks and I were on the bill. Heading into the event, I was as confident as ever—I might not have been the suavest, the strongest, or the godliest, but in rap battles, I felt unbeatable.

Until . . . I lost. In the final. To Lyricks. In front of an audience full of Koreans. It was embarrassing. His rhymes were better; his disses were sharper. At one point, he called me a "North Korean Super Mario Brother"—it might sound strange now, but in the moment, it killed in the room.

Mind you, this wasn't some blowout victory. I held my own.

But it was humbling, nonetheless. I was a Project Blowed alum in my hometown, losing a battle to a Christian rapper from fucking Virginia. I remember punching the air backstage, mentally replaying every line, furious that I'd lost. Thankfully—just like the footage of Eminem losing in the '97 Rap Olympics to Otherwize—you'll never see that battle between me and Lyricks on YouTube. Not because Dr. Dre found it and buried it, but because I told PK to keep it locked away forever. Petty, maybe, but I had a reputation to uphold.

Even if he was good at it, I don't think Lyricks had the temperament to continue battling as a career. He was always wrestling with the inner conflict between his Christian background and the decidedly un-Christian qualities you need to be a ruthless battler. I guess he was like J. Cole, in a way—an incredible rapper with depth and skill, but just not built for the arena.

Anyway, I started visiting Lyricks a lot in his Highland Park apartment to hang out, freestyle, and smoke weed. He shot my very first music video, for a song called "Bullets of Truth," and we've remained close friends and collaborators ever since. Through Lyricks, I met the homie who would end up being by my side for the formative years of my professional career. When Lyricks first moved to L.A., he brought a childhood friend from Virginia to be his roommate: Alessandro, better known as DJ Zo. Eventually, Lyricks needed to move back to Virginia, which was around the same time I was about to go on my first tour—and I invited Zo to come with me. So, I guess you could say my payback for losing the battle to Lyricks was stealing his DJ.

Rick is now making food-related content under the moniker Bap Ross—dude can eat as prolifically as he can rap. His food narrations are somewhere between Nas and Anthony Bourdain. He also ghostwrites for K-pop artists on the side.

In the end, he didn't just push me—he humbled me. If Nocando was the mentor who elevated my skills, Lyricks was the rival who made me reckon with my ego and showed me the value of mutual respect.

* * *

I admire these four MCs for their skills, but I'm paying homage to them not just for how they rap, but for how they influenced my journey as an artist. I studied the ups and downs of the rappers I saw on TV as well as the ones I knew in real life. They say never meet your heroes. Not only have I met most of mine, I've battled a bunch of them too. Each role model showed me a different way to do it in a world with no guidebook. But to master my own voice, I had to draw my own map.

CHAPTER FIVE

FREESTYLING & BATTLING FOR DUMMIES

People always ask me: "How do you freestyle? Like, how do you just start rhyming shit out of nowhere?" Rhymes fascinate kids from the moment they pick up a Dr. Seuss book. There is something inherently human about finding rhythms and patterns when you speak. Some of it you can practice—and believe me, I practiced *a lot.* But a big part of it is pure instinct, flow state, maybe even an out-of-body experience or divine intervention. It's a delicate balance between what you've trained for and what you're willing to let go of. It captures all the improvisational riffs of jazz, but with words. Controlled chaos. A trust fall into your own mind.

Then, there's the other question I get all the time: "What's it like standing toe-to-toe in a rap battle? How do you come up with insults that rhyme?" Well—that's where you take the improv skill from freestyling and sharpen it into a weapon. Then you point that weapon at an opponent and strike. You analyze their weak spots and target them. It's shooting the dozens, it's roasting, it's classroom taunting with rhythm and crowd control. To win, you must be savvy, clever, ruthless, and culturally fluent.

Freestyling and battling are complementary skills, requiring nimbleness, speed of thought, and the embodiment of Bruce Lee's philosophy of being like water—that's why they call it "flow." But being good at one doesn't automatically make you adept at the other. The common thread is that both are fueled by crowd approval. Eliciting the best reactions from a crowd has been my strongest motivator since day one.

So, I'll take a stab at answering those questions, using lessons I've picked up along the way. Every MC will have their own version of this process, but here's mine.

How to Go off the Top of the Dome

The ability to conjure rhymes off the top of the dome requires both tangible and intangible skills. Let's start with the tangible: You need the words to spit. Lots of them. If you're a true wordsmith, over time you'll accumulate a nearly unlimited word bank of rhymes through repetition and muscle memory. Remember my bus rides to school, when I'd reel off rhymes inspired by words I saw on random billboards? Later, in my teenage years, when I was roommates with fellow battle rapper Sahtyre, we'd turn basic convos into fuel for our rhyme addiction. I'd be like, "Yo, do the dishes," and he'd respond, "Your mom's bootylicious." I'd follow up with "eucalyptus" or "superstitious" or whatever sprang to mind. It was like hood *Hamilton.*

So how does one build a word bank? Well, let's take "word bank" itself. The first thing I think of is "sperm bank." (Yes, my mind's always in the gutter.) Then comes "Burbank," then I go to "third rank"—rhymes start dropping in my head like Tetris blocks.

Next, you have to make those blocks fit together. So, your job is to take the "word bank" stem, add new shoots and branches, and turn them into bars. Ask yourself: *How will I fill in the spaces between the rhymes so everything makes sense?* You can get clever with it, too, while thinking of the other connecting words. For example, "word bank" and "herb, dank." Picture me like Tom Cruise in *Minority Report*, but instead of rearranging holograms, I'm swiping through syllables in midair, frantically moving rhyme fragments around my head.

Deep in my word bank
Nutty, like a sperm bank
Fly, like the airport in Burbank
A general, you're only third rank
Smoke you like herb, dank

It's all supposed to sound random, like I'm conjuring these rhymes out of thin air, but in reality, my brain is in overdrive, choosing which direction my tongue will go.

Wanna try it yourself? I'll give you a pair of words: "book chapter." See if you can come up with a few rhyming phrases on the spot. Then try to put them together into a coherent rhyme scheme. A little more fun than Wordle, am I right?

When you have enough deposits in your word bank, you can accumulate a portfolio of premeditated rhymes to deploy in a pinch. For example, I always knew that whenever I joined a cypher, there was a good chance I would hear someone call me Jackie Chan. As a result, I stockpiled words that rhymed: "cans of spam," "handyman," "Amsterdam," "Hammer pants," and so on were collected like boxes of ammo stacked on mental shelves. In the early days, I'd hop into a cypher and play it off like I was freestyling—but most of my rhymes were premeditated phrases strung together.

After a while, I kept seeing and hearing rappers I looked up to freestyling—I mean *really* freestyling—and from the way the words flowed out, you could tell they were spinning them in real time. For example, Busdriver would connect wild thoughts like "magnanimous" and "bag of cannabis" and "panelist"—stuff no one else would ever conceive of rhyming. That excited me, because I'd hear it and think, *Damn, I don't think anyone on this planet has ever put those two things together.* So that became one of my goals, too: to rhyme words that no one has linked before.

To level up, you gotta take the hand brake off and fully let go. That's when you transcend premeditated lines and start floating like Aladdin on a carpet made of punchlines. Easier said than done. (Or is that easier done than said?) Psychologists talk about "internal" versus "external" processors. Internals organize their thoughts before they speak; externals blurt out what's on their mind and figure it out mid-sentence. Freestyling is like being 20 percent internal and 80 percent external. You've got the word bank in your head but the trick is organizing it while you're spitting, not before.

This brings us to one of the more intangible qualities you need to become an elite freestyler or elite at pretty much anything: *confidence*. In the freestyle context, it means not thinking too hard or getting into your own head, but at the same time thinking incredibly fast. In fact, you're thinking so fast that you're jumping to the next thought as quickly as the last one leaves your brain. You have to think, but you also must be willing to let the thoughts go as soon as they leave your mouth—that's the best way I can explain how to get in the zone. No time to celebrate a tight bar or dwell on a flub. Just keep going.

Then, rhyming words and phrases becomes a game. You get points for making words rhyme, and you get double points if you can make the connective parts in the middle a punchline too. As your verse unfolds, it's your brain, your mouth, and your vocabulary working together to collect rings like Sonic. Stringing together a long, uninterrupted streak of rhymes tickles the same nerve centers as flawlessly nailing a complicated solo on *Guitar Hero*. Gamifying a task has always been a mental cheat code for me to get better at something. The ultimate goal is to achieve a flow state, where each punchline just naturally comes. You're not mentally preparing the ending—somehow the universe hands it to you. In that zone, you're not thinking about your last word or even the next one. You let your mouth feel the last rhyme and trust it to deliver the next. The words on your tongue lead, you follow them into the pocket, and somehow it all connects. Let go fully, and you practically enter another dimension. Every elite freestyler knows that feeling, even if they describe it differently. Eminem once said in Ice-T's *The Art of Rap* documentary that it's like solving a puzzle—each word is a piece you need to fit into place. The late Juice WRLD compared it to freehand drawing a masterpiece, as opposed to tracing an outline. And Supernatural, one of the greatest of them all, said that a freestyle is "the highest form of expression through one's self." For me, it was all these things: puzzle, painting, and portal to another realm.

Of course, it takes practice to get there. After witnessing Blowed, I was spending nearly every waking hour getting my reps in, diving fully into my obsession. I'd be at home, skipping school, smoking weed, and freestyling—not only feeling myself getting better, but also getting better reactions from whoever was around. Beyond the weed, I got a natural body high from freestyling. It felt like being in a drum circle in Venice Beach—I was exerting myself physically, but in rhythm, tapping into something collective and ancient.

Here's a bonus question I get from time to time: "Are you better at freestyling when you're dead sober or when you're drunk or high?" Well, to be clear: Drunk freestyles, stoned freestyles, and coked-out freestyles each have a different feel. (Note: People often ply freestyle rappers with various substances at parties and events because they think it's a performance enhancer.) When you're drunk, the liquor may pump your tires and convince you that you're killing it, but in reality, you usually end up slurring and spitting on people. On weed, you start to get more experimental, transforming into a freestyle wizard, which can either be really dope or really draining. When people talk about "lyrical miracles," that's what they're talking about. (Sometimes in battles, even when I'm not stoned, I act stoned—it lowers expectations.) And coke? It makes your heart beat a hundred miles per hour; your hands get sweaty, and you're suddenly louder and more aggressive, but not necessarily better. In my younger years, I did a lot of battling on coke. If you watch my two-on-two World Rap Championships battles alongside Sahtyre in 2007, you'll see both of us touching our noses throughout the competition.

All intoxicants make you feel tighter than you actually are. But whether sober or high, I feel like freestyles should live and die in the moment. Part of their mystique is that they are so ephemeral. It's why I feel people shouldn't record and rewatch freestyles. They should exist in real time, when everyone within earshot gets to experience it and react organically. When you rewatch cyphers, it's often way wacker than you remember. Freestyling at Blowed was special because fewer people were recording back then—if anyone was recording, they had to lug around an actual camcorder. You can't recreate that feeling anymore.

But in the modern era, once you start freestyling in a public setting, everything is on the record. This is especially true of rap battles, a content industry in its own right. It's not only about the words you say, but what viewers see when you walk up to the mic.

How to Roast and Read the Room

Here's a little thought exercise: What are the top five ways you could insult an Asian guy? (If you're Asian, you probably won't have to think too hard; if you're not Asian, don't worry, you won't get canceled.)

Got them in mind? Good. Now let's review.

Most likely, within your list are the following commonly held stereotypes:

1. Asians have small, slanted eyes; Asian men have small dicks.
2. Asians can't drive.
3. Asians eat cats and dogs.
4. Asians are nerds who are good at math.
5. All Asians look alike.

Surprise, surprise. The stereotypes above are also the most common battle insults I've heard as an Asian rapper. As I started to take battling to a national level, facing off against people from all over the country, I began noticing that all my opponents had very limited knowledge of Asian people. I knew this because I was getting hit with these same tired stereotypes over and over again. (Sad part is, some of these jokes still draw big laughs from the audience.)

While we're here, let me quickly debunk these myths, along with actual quotes from my battles to illustrate how they can be used.

1. Asians have small, slanted eyes; Asian men have small dicks.

Yo, look at your fucking moon shaped, Lucy Liu face /
Your dick is like a half-used tube of toothpaste —Dizaster (2015)

The eye thing is the lowest-hanging fruit of anti-Asian insults, a go-to since the "coolies" were building American railroads in the mid-nineteenth century. Nearly two hundred years later, "almond-shaped eyes" are weirdly fetishized when it's convenient—just look at K-beauty trends or white chicks biting eyeliner tips from Asian makeup influencers.

As for dick size—ayo!—a 2015 study, published in the *BJU International Journal of Urology*, analyzed 15,000 penises from around the world and determined no evidence that penis size differences were linked to race. (I cannot confirm whether or not it was Asian researchers who conducted this study.)

2. Asians can't drive.

I'm something you can't pass, like a North Korean border sniper's nest / Or a driver's test —Kid Twist (2009)

We've all heard the rhyme: "Asian driver, no survivor." If not, I'm sorry for introducing it to you. I'm befuddled how we earned the stereotype of being bad drivers. I just don't get it. Most of the cars on American roads are from Asia (no fewer than sixteen of the top twenty-five cars sold in 2024 were from Asian brands). We obviously know cars. Look at Han in *The Fast and Furious*. To be fair, it's mostly Asian women who get unfairly hit with the stereotype—which I get because I was a passenger in my mom's car for many years—but why does it apply to all of us? The stats don't back it up. According to the Governors Highway Safety Association, Asian individuals have a significantly lower per-capita rate of total traffic fatalities compared to other racial groups. If anything, we're *too* cautious on the road. Our good driving drives people crazy.

3. Asians eat cats and dogs.

When it's raining cats and dogs / You run outside with packs of sauce —The Saurus (2007)

Ah, the classic. Yes, there are rural communities in various Asian countries which have, uh, different relationships with animals. But while dietary customs vary globally, nearly all Asian Americans adhere to the same cultural norms regarding pets as other Americans. Somehow, Donald Trump co-opted this stereotype and turned it on Haitian immigrants in Ohio during the 2024 presidential campaign. Fuck outta here. I mean, have you ever investigated exactly what's inside your glizzy?

4. Asians are nerds who are good at math.

I'll beat your ass /
Like a Korean dad /
When you bring home a B in math. —Nocando (2005)

Sheeeeeeeeee-it, I wish this were true for me. Would've helped out a lot at John Marshall High. Anyway, this one seems like a compliment—until you realize it's used to flatten us into the whole "model minority" trap. It might've been part of the reason why Andrew Yang couldn't rally Asian Americans like me with his ill-fated 2020 presidential campaign. You'd never catch me rocking a hat that said "MATH" on it, fam.

Anyway, Asian American students do, on average, score higher in eighth-grade math assessments than their counterparts of other ethnicities. But that's not genetic or some innate ability—it's environmental (tiger moms and dads), cultural (emphasis on education and study habits), and sometimes survival-based. Mastering calculus is our version of having a wicked jump shot. If any of those boxes are left unchecked, like they were for me, you're definitely not winning any math competitions. Or wearing a MATH hat.

5. All Asians look alike.

Which one of y'all is Dumbfoundead? /
*Both of you n*ggas look alike* —Conceited (2015)

When I was coming up, I would get compared to the only three Asian people that people usually know: Jackie Chan, Jet Li, and Bruce Lee. (Of course, times have changed now and there's at least one or two non-martial artists that they can reference—thank you, Steven Yeun and BTS.) The whole "I can't tell y'all apart" bit is ignorant when referring to the vast diaspora of people hailing from the largest continent, with over 4.5 billion people across more than fifty countries—each with distinct ethnicities, cultures, and physical features. To be fair, I couldn't tell the difference between all the white people on *Game of Thrones*.

The purpose of this exercise is not for me to get defensive about stereotypes, but to illustrate what an Asian American has to deal with in the field of battle rap. (And, more broadly speaking, what any non-Black artist in this arena has to face.) As a matter of fact, my very first experience was fending off a race-related insult. Flashback to lunchtime during my freshman year at John Marshall: I was huddled up with a group of kids at a table freestyling when a Latino kid spit a rhyme targeted at me: *I chew up these rappers like Juicy Fruit / Shout-out to the homie here lookin' like Lucy Liu*. (Is that better or worse than being called Jackie Chan?)

There's an old Dave Chappelle stand-up bit where he talks about the 2006 incident when Michael Richards, aka Kramer from *Seinfeld*, was onstage at the Laugh Factory and started yelling the N-word at Black people in the crowd. Chappelle quipped that when he saw the footage, he knew he was 20 percent Black and 80 percent comedian because although he was pissed, his main thought was: *Whew, he's having a bad set!*

I mention that to say this: The moment I got called Lucy Liu, I realized I was wired to be 20 percent Asian and 80 percent battle rapper. Because instead of taking offense, I thought, *Damn that was pretty good—think of something fast, Jonnie, don't embarrass yourself.* I immediately hit him with: *Yeah, bitch, I am Lucy Liu / I'll twist your neck like a Rubik's Cube / And put my foot in your ass without using lube.* The table erupted. It was the first—but definitely not the last—time I had to flip a racial joke on its head and weaponize it.

Now, for a quick distinction between the different variants of battle rap:

- **Diss tracks.** This is classic rap history, like KRS-One versus MC Shan, Canibus versus LL, Nas versus Jay-Z, and of course, Drake versus Kendrick Lamar. (More on that one later.) Rappers record songs dissing each other and release them. I've never actually recorded one.
- **Freestyle battles.** Like the Lucy Liu example above, this is classic cafeteria shit, usually over a beat that's literally handmade off the lunch table or by someone beatboxing. This also applies to the countless off-the-top battles I participated in at Project Blowed cyphers: actual freestyles with targeted, on-the-fly insults at whoever happens to be in the vicinity. Freestyle battles are a lost art now—basically just a cool party trick.
- **Freestyle battles over beats.** Like what you saw in *8 Mile*—a DJ plays an instrumental, and two MCs go at it, mixing (mostly) prewritten rhymes with some off-the-top responses to react to whatever's happening in the moment.

- **A cappella battles.** The modern form of battle rap, where two opponents are matched up in advance and prepare their rhymes accordingly—like boxers training before a televised prizefight. This is like a sport, organized by groups like Grind Time, King of the Dot, and Ultimate Rap League—and how I made my name.

Back to stereotyping: When I battled opponents from different ethnicities and backgrounds, I also sometimes caught myself resorting to stereotypes—so it also taught me about my own ignorance. Ultimately, the goal is to get to a punchline, and the best ones subvert the audience's expectations.

That's the irony of using stereotypes effectively in battle raps. In order to diss an opponent properly, you have to respect and study their culture. It's how a comedian can get away with what may sound like offensive jokes—by exhibiting an understanding of their nuances. When Indian Canadian comedian Russell Peters performed jokes about different kinds of Asians, it worked because you could tell he grew up around Chinese and Filipino kids. So, if I'm battling a Latino dude, I need to reference specific cultural elements, not just generic shit like tacos and burritos. Growing up, I was the only Asian kid on my block nicknamed Chino; I participated in a quinceañera. I dated girls with cholo uncles and knew that chapín was a slang term for Guatemalans. I could distinguish between a Guatemalan and a Salvadoran and knew about their cultural beefs. These are specific things only someone who grew up with Latinos would know, so when I used this stuff in battles, the Latinos watching were like, "Oh, this guy isn't just dropping stereotypes, he gets it."

Having that kind of cultural awareness helps you gain the crowd's respect.

When I battled Latino rapper Illusion-Z in 2009, my angle was to get the largely Latino crowd on my side—you could say I was like Trump trying to win the Latino vote. But unlike Donald, I had authenticity on my side, because I grew up with Latinos my entire life.

To gain credibility with the audience, I made references to classic Chicano films and mixed in some Spanish.

You were in the cast of Blood In Blood Out
You have seventeen cousins, one house
Yell "La Migra!" and watch more than a dozen run out

I also worked the angle of him being a whitewashed Latino.

I don't care if you're bilingual, he came to L.A. tryna mingle
But doesn't feel safe unless he's around five gringos

Trust me, I got love for Latinos, but no love for you
And they like me a lot more, which sucks for you
And you know what's funny, too?
You're the only guy at a quinceañera at age twenty-two

And once the crowd was on my side, I twisted the knife with a clever flip of a stereotype.

Lookin' like a sherm addict
You ain't even Hispanic, you a Her-spanic
Someone throw a purse at him
And out of everyone who battle raps, you're the worst at it
How the fuck do you have lazy work habits? You're Spanish!

Despite how that last line might read on paper, the crowd ate it up.

Circling back to the Asian stereotypes list: In Jin's Freestyle Friday run, his opponents failed because they mostly relied on tired Asian jokes that didn't challenge or impress the audience. Like, *Yo, I'm a star, he just a rookie / Leave rap alone and keep making fortune cookies.* Gong. Jin's foes weren't culturally aware enough to trouble him or win the judges over.

The truth remains, however, that people still find racist Asian jokes a lot funnier than those about other races. I've battled dudes who came dressed as Buddhist monks, pulling their eyes slanted, performing high kicks, even throwing invisible Hadoukens like on *Street Fighter.* I admit that it can sting when the crowd cheers so hard for bullshit stunts like that. I'm thinking, *Shit was corny;* meanwhile, the audience is roaring its approval. It's not that any particular insult is hurtful to me; it's that everybody watching eats it up. So, I'm left thinking, *Oh shit, I was wrong—that stuff still works.* It's bigger than hip-hop, obviously. Battle rap is like a pressure cooker for the racism that already exists in society. The same stereotypes from the outside world don't just appear; they come out rawer and harder with a rabid crowd egging them on.

That's why it hits different when you hear an Asian jab that has a level of intelligence attached to it. I refer back to when Serius Jones told Jin, *You been wack your whole career / Ain't it two billion people in China? / You can't even go platinum over there!* Serius used Jin's ethnicity as a baseline for the rhyme, acknowledging China's massive population. But the best battle punchlines aren't offensive to an entire group of people; they're only offensive to *you.*

The other element of battle rap that elevates it beyond basic taunting or even stand-up is that it's not just the material—it's also the rhythm and the rhyme. A good rhyme can make anything sound great. When things are said in rhyme, it just feels good. Like the time I battled The Saurus, and he ended his round with "Good morning, Vietnam!" The crowd didn't go wild because he was referring to a long-forgotten eighties movie with Robin Williams—they went apeshit because his setup was so tight.

Bring me a plate of freaking sushi
Which would normally be wrong
But I need more to feed upon than your poor Korean mom
I woke up to her pleasuring me orally at dawn
Opened both my eyes and shouted, "Good morning, Vietnam!"

If you have great rhymes, it's gonna hit regardless. (It's unfortunate that "Bruce Lee" rhymes perfectly with "sushi," since those are probably two of the top ten Asian references in the world. And don't get me started on "Kristi Yamaguchi.")

I've battled pretty much every race under the sun, and some of the hardest dudes to beat were nerdy white dudes. White people have a natural instinct for getting goofy as fuck. I remember taking improv classes at Upright Citizens Brigade for the first time in my early twenties, and I was the only Asian—actually, the only nonwhite—person there. The instructor's prompt was something about "gay pirates," and these white guys just jumped forward and started prancing around and giggling like flamboyant Jack Sparrows. Watching them, I realized there was a cultural element to the freedom white people have, where that kind of silly role play is encouraged. The entitlement comes from its long history in American pop culture. For me? Improv class was uncomfortable because I'm coming from cyphers, Blowed, and hip-hop (plus an extremely unfunny father). I didn't want to act like a gay pirate, because I was irrationally paranoid that somehow the homies would bust in and see me. Ayo . . . I mean, ahoy.

Next to Asians, nerdy white dudes are the most clowned-on in pop culture. The jokes have all been done: pocket protectors, glasses, no game. So, most white nerds lean into the persona—once again, the *8 Mile* Eminem effect—and wear it when they step into the arena. They beat everyone to the punch by accepting it. They also have the built-in advantage of lowered expectations. Anything even slightly good that leaves a nerdy white dude's mouth in a battle is going to shock people. And they can be extremely clever. What they lack in rhythm and "coolness," they try to make up for with researched bars and multisyllabic rhymes.

An opponent's immutable characteristics are only the entry point; you must draw the map to attack the target. In 2023, when I came back from hiatus to battle Rone—a pretty regular, somewhat nerdy white dude who works for Barstool Sports—I tied his whiteness to college frat dudes, which let me call him a date rapist, and then a racist, and suddenly he's storming the Capitol on January 6. I painted him as this ignorant white bro, culture-vulture character, even if he's not—he's actually a friend of mine. Interesting note about the Rone battle: When I called him a right-wing Trump supporter, not everyone rocked with me because it turns out MAGA has infected even battle-rap fans. After all, they both love shock value and insults as entertainment.

By far the hardest opponent to battle is regular-looking Black dudes (which makes Jin's triumphs all the more impressive). There's no doubt that this is their sport. They rightfully hold home-court advantage. (However, I imagine that Black MCs have their own hurdles, because unlike nerdy white or Asian rappers, they can't really rely on that *8 Mile* "I'll clown myself before you do" tactic.) Ultimately, winning a battle has nothing to do with physical stature or voice or delivery. It's about the material and the rhymes. And when I'm going up against a Black opponent, I would never resort to a joke about fried chicken or watermelon or blackface. That stuff might work in a comedy roast, but rap battles are about saying things more cleverly and indirectly. Calling a Black man a deadbeat dad, for example, will hit more at a roast or an episode of *Kill Tony* than in a battle—that's a very white approach. Nobody is going to get on your side in a battle if you crack a joke like that. You gotta find another angle. Something more personal like height, weight, age, hygiene . . . or just start making up fake facts.

Look at Kendrick Lamar and Drake, for example. Kendrick leaned into a narrative about Drake being a pedophile. Sure, Kendrick had bars about Drake being biracial or having weird friends, but a lot of people are biracial and have weird friends. Everybody hates pedophilia—it's indefensible. It is undefeated in terms of offensiveness.

Drake tried to rebut with domestic violence allegations, but that still doesn't beat pedophilia. Kendrick found the top of the insult pyramid. Also, Drake had much more material online for Kendrick to work with. On a much smaller scale, I could relate. At some point in my later years, it got dangerous for me to battle because I have a larger digital footprint than most people. (As a quick example, I was on a video podcast with Bobby Lee and his brother Steve, and we all showed our asses—literally—and were judged on who had the best butt. Anything for content, yeah?)

Personally, I don't like to include anything in a battle that requires heavy research. I attribute a big part of my success to the fact that anyone could watch one of my battles and pick up exactly what's going on without context. I'm not gonna mention an obscure police file my opponent had five years ago and why he served time. I want your mom to be able to watch the battle and laugh at what I'm saying.

To bring it back full circle: We all play into racial stereotypes, and even when you're responding to one lobbed at you, you're reinforcing it. It starts to feel irresponsible to even dignify a dog-eating joke by playing off of it. The way Jin phrased a lot of his rounds on Freestyle Friday was cool then, but to do that now just seems like a crutch. It actually creates an opening for others to join in on the joke, the way Chappelle talked about how his Comedy Central show was giving non-Black people an opening to make fun of them. By embracing a stereotype *too* hard, you unintentionally give others permission to pile on. Not to get too deep about rap battling, but while I'm targeting my opponent, I also want to challenge the audience—to make them dig deeper into what I'm saying. That's the difference between low-hanging fruit and actual art.

In hip-hop, it's of paramount importance to gain approval from your Black peers, which is why I think a lot of new-school Asian rappers go extra hard on their Asianness, almost making caricatures of themselves. They're out here doing YouTube cyphers literally holding a bowl of noodles and spitting, *I'm the hardest chink*. But who is this shtick even for? I think it's partly meant for other Asians, to clear out space from the competition, but that is a zero-sum mentality. It's the same feeling I had growing up, when I was the only Asian in my crew, and suddenly I saw a new Asian kid move in—I felt threatened, like they were coming for my space, and I had to defend it. Going extra hard and outlandish is also cultural residue for Asians, in that we come from a culture of *not* doing that. Since the majority of Asians aren't saying unhinged stuff, we overcompensate by saying the wildest shit we can think of.

It's funny how becoming a renowned battle rapper has actually brought me closer to my Asian roots. Even though I may not have fully known what it meant to be Asian, I knew the names I was being called barely scratched the surface of what being Asian is all about. Once I started winning, all the Asian kids in my neighborhood and all over the country who once alienated me were in my corner, thanking me for representing and holding it down for our people.

The twist is—because the universe has a sense of humor—I built my rep defending Asians in battles and then blew up worldwide by destroying one.

CHAPTER SIX

THERE CAN BE ONLY ONE

Dumbfoundead vs. Tantrum, 2008

I almost missed the rap battle that changed my life because, as usual, I was running late. Maybe deep down I *wanted* to miss it, because of nerves, or because I felt unprepared, or self-sabotage. Either way, it was the most important battle—strike that, the most important event—of my life up to that point. It was a clash against Tantrum, the rival who had become the yin to my yang.

In defense of my lateness, I wasn't traveling alone. Packed inside my raggedy Ford Focus were five of the eight members of my Swim Team crew—Lyraflip, Sahtyre, Open Mike Eagle, Psychosiz, and me—for the roughly six-hour drive from L.A. to Oakland. It was Saturday, November 15, and I was driving us to an event called the Battle of the Bay 2. I entered the competition with no shortage of confidence. I might've been struggling to break through as a full-time artist, but I'd been winning battles left and right across L.A. People knew my name.

Still, I felt my nerves building as we pulled up to the corner of

Broadway and West MacArthur. The Oakland battle would present an entirely different challenge than what I was used to, for a couple of reasons. First, it would be my first solo a cappella battle, using prewritten, memorized rhymes, not going off the top. Up to that point, all my battles were freestyled over beats, like the shit they did in *8 Mile*. This new format, which would soon turn battle rap into a pay-per-view sport like boxing, required planning, practice, and strategy. Even more significant was the identity of my opponent: a Chinese American rapper from the Bay Area named Tantrum. For the first time ever, two Asian Americans would be going head-to-head in a big-time battle.

I had slayed any number of Asian rappers in impromptu battles over the years. This, however, was part of a bill promoted by Grind Time Now, one of the premier battle-rap leagues. When they asked me to participate, I saw their vision. I knew it was going to do numbers. Tantrum and I were similar in age—he was twenty-five, I was twenty-two—but other than that, we were polar opposites. We were both protégés of Scribble Jam champs. He came up under The Saurus, the multisyllabic king; I came up under Nocando, the witty street scholar. He repped the Bay; I repped L.A. Tantrum's style, true to his name, was angry and confrontational, like DMX if he drove a souped-up Acura Integra. I was a sarcastic asshole. With our clashing styles, it promised to be an entertaining bout.

Everything I'd seen and experienced in life set me up to conquer Tantrum. I was ready. I knew all the Asian angles. I knew how we thought, what jokes touched our nerves. I also knew how to weaponize Asian punchlines that non-Asian people—the majority of the crowd—would respond to. But that was hardly an advantage; Tantrum could probably say the same exact thing. He also lived life as an Asian American and knew the same angles I did. Usually, being the only Asian in a battle meant I stood out. This time, I wasn't the token; I was the mirror. Sigmund Freud called it "the narcissism of small differences": the idea that, ironically, the more similar you are to someone, the more animosity you'll have toward that person. It becomes an existential crisis when a person who resembles you comes along and threatens your uniqueness. A line from the movie *Highlander* said it in a much catchier way than Freud: There can be only one.

My first nickname growing up was "Chino," because I was the one Asian face in a Latino crew. I loved the moniker—it felt like I got jumped into a Mexican gang. The attention I got for being an outlier gave me a sense of identity. It made me feel special . . . until I met another Asian kid a couple blocks over. When I introduced myself as Chino, he replied, sneering, "But *I'm* Chino, fool." It was the Spider-Man meme come to life, except it was two Mexican-acting Korean dudes pointing at each other. I then realized that every Asian person in L.A. is a "Chino" to somebody.

As an Asian American in rap, I've dealt with some annoying insults, but I never saw my outsider status as a disadvantage. Again, being uncommon makes you stand out. It puts you in a league of your own. That's why I immediately tensed up when I met Lyricks and saw how good he was at rapping. It felt like he was coming to take my spot as *the* Asian American rapper, a title I had fought so hard to attain. If you want to get deep into how white supremacy affects us all, this kind of scarcity mindset pits people of color in a deathmatch for scraps of opportunity instead of taking a step back and asking how to make the pie bigger for everyone. Like crabs in a barrel, if I rise, someone else must fall.

Pitted against another Asian American MC, my competitive instincts kicked in harder than I'd ever felt before. Call it some Freudian shit or a *Highlander* callback or whatever you want, but on both a conscious and subconscious level, I just could not tolerate another Asian rapper challenging my superiority—and I'm pretty sure Tantrum felt the exact same way. That autumn night, I showed up to Mosswood Park in a black T-shirt with L.A. across the front, proudly repping my hometown for an away game in Oakland. The park was full of people, some of whom knew me for my freestyle battles but had no idea what to expect from me in the new prewritten, a cappella format. As the start time approached, murmurs spread through the crowd as people circled around Tantrum and me. The host, Lush One, a Mexican-looking white guy wearing a fitted cap and T-shirt that were both two sizes too big, mock-bowed to the camera like a kung-fu master to kick things off, which got laughs from the audience.

I had a leg up from jump because I won the coin toss and made Tantrum go first. My belief is that having the last word is always an advantage. (Funny enough, I don't think I won another coin toss my entire battle career.) When he started spitting, his rabid-dog aggression didn't surprise me—I had seen his battles before—but in person, with his hands flailing in my face, it was much more visceral than I'd anticipated. I could see the veins in his neck bulge every time he barked "fuck" or "bitch" at the top of his lungs. Strangely, the angry energy he exuded in the first round calmed my nerves. It confirmed my pre-game strategy. The calmer I stayed, the more he would look like a tryhard.

Still, it wasn't like Tantrum was bombing. He predictably attacked me for being nerdy and soft, but what impressed me was the specificity of his Asian references. He dropped a *Highlander* "the one" reference in his opening four bars before going deep into his Asian bag:

This video game freak went stark mad for Dragon Quest
Your parents had to cut your allowance and leave your narc ass with half a cent
'Cause you spent all your hard cash on the StarCraft *expansion set*
What? You think you can flow, dog? 'Cause you fucking with the Protoss?

The line about *StarCraft*, the 1990s PC game beloved by Koreans, hit hard, but he went even further, name-dropping Protoss, one of the three species in the game. Once Tantrum started leaning into deep-cut Asian lore, I realized we were in the same headspace. Ironically, by trying to call me a nerd through obscure video-game references, he came off nerdier. (To this day, I still don't know what *Dragon Quest* is.) It put me at ease, even if the crowd was feeling him, because I was confident that my Asian bars would resonate better. I knew exactly how nerdy I could get without losing the room.

When I started my first rebuttal, I could immediately feel a shift in energy from the unhinged rants of a madman to the low-key, biting commentary of a comic. I was relaxed, channeling a stoner vibe although I hadn't smoked. I dove straight into the comparison bars—*While I was attending funerals and smoking chron / You was playing* Yu-Gi-Oh! *and* Pokémon—that would become my battle trademark. (I would cater this tactic to my opponent. For example, against an older MC: *I used to play* Super Mario Brothers *in the arcade / You used to play* Super Mario Brothers, *the board game.*)

Everything in that first round was hitting, but I knew the crowd was on my side after I dropped these bars:

I was getting paid and laid by tens
You was acting gay and go raved with friends
Dropping ecstasy without pants
Doing some weird-ass house dance wearin' Mickey Mouse hands

Once I said "Mickey Mouse hands," sending the audience into hysterics, even Tantrum had to turn his head to conceal a laugh. It was the perfect, comically relatable image that touched on a specific subset of Asian Americans yet was instantly understood by everybody. After that first round, I was pretty sure I had the battle in the bag.

Tantrum didn't go down without a fight, though. He elicited the strongest crowd reaction of the night with this:

Even in here there's segregation
I'm faster at solving test equations, basically I'm just a better Asian
See I spit sicker and I rhyme fresher
I can kick quicker by a high measure
And just to throw it in, my dick's bigger and I drive better

Nevertheless, bar for bar, I just had too many sharp jokes that landed. And I saved my best for the end of the third round, probably the bars people remember most from the entire battle:

I don't even know why the fuck I'm battling this panhandling
Mandarin Asian
You used to manhandle pandas in cages for gambling wagers
In conclusion, Tantrum's a hater
Didn't anybody tell you those pants are for ravers?
How ironic, you just got served in Oakland by a Los Angeles Raider

The finish landed like a death blow because it was delivered on his home turf.

Postscript: The three judges unanimously voted me the winner. Weeks later, the battle was posted on WorldStarHipHop.com, which was then the most popular rap video site. The duel spread like wildfire. I knew it was getting big when L.A. rap legends like The Alchemist and Evidence called to congratulate me. Unreal. Soon after, the vibe in Koreatown changed. Asian gangsters who used to bully me started to show me love. The same dudes who once roasted me for my scruffy hair, skater shirts, and ripped Dickies were now dapping me up and trying to take pictures with me. To this day, if someone knows me from battle rap, it's most likely because they saw that battle.

When I rewatch the footage now, I see that my performance was a bit messy and rushed. It was my first a capella battle, and I wasn't yet used to the different rhythm of a battle without an instrumental. When rhyming over music, if you bomb a line, you can kind of hide behind the drums and keep it moving. Conversely, a great line can get lost in the beat. Without backing music, you feel the silence if a line doesn't work, but you also soak in the sound of the crowd's

"Dumbfoundead vs. Tantrum"
Art by Turtleboat

YOU WERE RACING *INTEGRAS AND HONDA CIVICS.*

藤原とうふ店

KANSAI DRIFT?!

I WAS GETTING PAID AND LAID BY TENS,

YOU WAS ACTING GAY AND *GO RAVED WITH FRIENDS,*

DROPPING ECSTASY WITHOUT PANTS, DOING SOME WEIRDASS HOUSE DANCE *WEARIN' MICKEY MOUSE HANDS.*

CHECK THIS OUT YALL, I'M A MIND READER,
CALL DUMBFOUNDEAD NOW,
1-800-212-
TANTRUM'S TANK-TOPS
YOU'RE THINKING ABOUT OPENING UP A DRY CLEANERS, THAT SPECIALIZES IN WIFE BEATERS,
YO WE GOTTA PRESS THESE TANK-TOPS FASTER!

I DON'T EVEN KNOW WHY I'M BATTLING THIS PANHANDLING MANDARIN ASIAN...
SOME CHANGE, GOOD SIR?

...YOU USED TO MANHANDLE PANDAS IN CAGES FOR GAMBLING WAGERS!

WAAAAAA!!
EVERYTHING THAT I HAD SEEN AND EXPERIENCED IN MY LIFE SET ME UP TO CONQUER THAT TANTRUM BATTLE.
I WAS READY. I KNEW ALL OF THE ASIAN ANGLES. I KNEW HOW WE THOUGHT; I KNEW WHAT JOKES TOUCHED OUR NERVES.

WHAT THE HELL DUDE, STOP *RAPPING* AND GO *SELL SHOES!*
AFTER YOU LOSE THIS BATTLE,
URRG

YOU'LL GO TO YOUR DAD AND GET DOWN ON YOUR *KNEES AND SAY,*
KGHH... I HAVE FAILED YOU!
DOO DOOM

approval when something hits. It's important to pace and time your cadence with the crowd reaction, but against Tantrum, I don't think I let my best punchlines settle before moving on to the next one.

As for Tantrum, I feel he could've gotten more specific with his ethnic taunts and targeted Korean culture the way I focused on his Chinese background (or maybe in the pre-BTS and *Parasite* world of 2008, there was less Korean culture in America to mock). Either way, the standoff between a shaggy Korean American joker and a shaved-headed Chinese American bully, seen in real time in Oakland and by millions online afterward, proved that Asian America is not a monolith. Now put that in your Asian American Studies syllabus.

I haven't spoken to him since, but I've seen on Instagram that he's still making music. Tantrum, if you're reading this, thank you for your part in a legendary battle. It helped my career in ways I can't even quantify. We made history together—even if I won.

CHAPTER SEVEN

BATTLE SCARS

After the Tantrum battle, the doors blew wide open. The victory put me on the map in a scene that was rapidly evolving. YouTube turned what were once local showcases into spectacles that could go viral overnight. Instead of signing up at the door to battle whoever showed up, I was getting booked in advance to take on specific opponents. The stage was getting bigger, and the stakes were getting higher.

I was strategic in the opponents I faced. Since I'd already defeated an Asian dude, I wanted to tackle other genres of rappers. My goal was to create a diverse catalog—my own Criterion Collection of battles. So, I battled a Latino dude. I battled an old dude. I battled a gun-toting dude. I battled a frat dude. If there was a box, I felt the need to check it. None of this was by coincidence; each adversary forced me to come up with new material.

What follows is a selection of my favorites. Be forewarned: Battle rap isn't for the thin-skinned. There exists a raw honesty that combines the harshest elements of hip-hop and comedy. I've said some cancelable shit in my battles—the F-word, the R-word (though never the N-word), and plenty of ethnic insults—but in those moments, the goal was to win. And, of course, I've had just as many thrown back at me. Nobody is immune, nothing is off the table. That's the nature of the sport. In its own twisted way, accepting that truth is how empathy can grow.

Below is the timeline: battle by battle, opponent by opponent, with my angles of attack and some of the best lines from either side. These face-offs demanded fresh bars delivered with precision, because one flub could be fatal. Winners and losers were determined informally, often inconclusively—some by a trio of judges, others left to fan reaction. I had a few decisive wins and a couple tough losses. But every single battle has a story behind it.

Date: January 24, 2009

Location: South Central L.A.

Opponent: Illusion-Z, a twenty-one-year-old Ecuadorian American from Stockton, CA

Angle of Attack: Diss him for being a whitewashed suburban Latino

My Best Bars:

Around here, you'll get blown to smithereens
You look like one of them 25-cent Homies figurines
I know you're not Mexican, but Imma still use Mexican jokes
You're Ecuadorean, that's like comparing Pepsi to Coke

His Best Bars:

I told my dog not to talk to this stranger
'Cause he's the main reason why my chihuahua's in danger

'Cause everytime I go to walk it at night
You stalk behind us with a wok and a knife

This battle came only two months after Tantrum, so people wanted to see me recreate that viral magic against a non-Asian opponent. Illusion-Z was an up-and-comer who'd recently bodied my Swim Team brother Lyraflip, so this felt like a kung-fu movie where I had to avenge the crew. It was the Bay versus L.A., Ecuador versus Korea, Latino versus Latino-adjacent (me). I think I did Flip justice.

Date: February 28, 2009

Location: Oakland, CA

Opponent: The Saurus, a twenty-seven-year-old from Monterey Bay, CA, and one of the GOATs of battle rap

Angle of Attack: Roast him with acne jokes and Greek nerd insults

My Best Bars:

I already beat the Asian and Latino versions of you, ya big loser
You can send all the Goombas you want, King Koopa
'Cause I'm the future of the West Coast, in L.A. we been mobbin'
I'll admit you gave birth to a lot of battle rappers, but they'll all have skin problems

His Best Bars:

Before the battle with Illusion
He was drinking tea, practicing Hadoukens
Yo, I want to punch the face of this guy, but based on the shape of his eyes
We know the policy, "You break it, you buy"

I was climbing the ranks fast, building enough clout to be a headliner. My next test was a heavyweight battle against a two-time Scribble Jam winner. Greek American Peter Morris, aka The Saurus, was a master of intricate, dense rhymes that played as well on YouTube as they did in the room. I'd admired him for years, so I came prepared with what I thought was witty material. However, my entire second round—themed around book titles—didn't quite capture the crowd. Meanwhile, The Saurus leaned heavily on stereotypical Asian jokes, but wove them into masterfully crafted punchlines, so they killed. The "Good Morning, Vietnam!" first-round closer—see Chapter Five—detonated the building. After that, I knew I was fighting uphill.

Date: April 18, 2009

Location: L.A.

Opponent: F.L.O., a twenty-nine-year-old Oakland comedian with effortless Bay swag

Angle of Attack: Out-funny him with weight and hygiene jokes

My Best Bars:

You're weaker than that one kid I served from Ecuador
I went from battling that last guy with infected pores
To some random dude no one's checking for

Looking like a musty, crusty, Bun B
You need lotion, ChapStick, and sunscreen
You look unhealthy and unclean

Ayo, not to mention, your body odor—someone spray some potpourri
He look like one of them fat, Black lesbian rappers, Imma call him F.L.O.etry

His Best Bars:

When I move to a neighborhood, the women stay wet
A week after you moved in, there wasn't no mo' stray pets
See you'll play rock paper scissors for chopped liver and potstickers
And eat a whole living catfish, even the eyes and whiskers

You a Southern Cali malnutritioned boy who lost
Whose biggest decision is between duck and soy sauce
Look, how come that, Mr. Chow Yun Fat
Can't tell the difference between cow or cat?

I opened with blatant disrespect: *I went from battling The Saurus to F.L.O. / what am I doing with my life?* But F.L.O. was no pushover. As an experienced comic, he knew how to work a crowd. Rocking white shades, F.L.O. dropped punchline after punchline with a laid-back cadence, like a Bay Area Mitch Hedberg. Humor was my strong suit too, so this was one of the funniest back-and-forths I'd ever had. In the end, I edged him out on sheer jokes per minute.

Date: September 5, 2009

Location: Oakland, CA

Opponent: PH, aka Pumpkinhead, a thirty-four-year-old OG in the NYC underground scene

Angle of Attack: Crack on his age and insult him about his career

My Best Bars:

I'm gonna explain to y'all how big this generation gap is
I was recently in the Fresh Coast *DVD bonus features*
You were in Wild Style *when it was shown in theaters*
He rocks throwback jerseys, not 'cause he's trying to

When he originally bought those, those players were kinda new
I used to play Super Mario Brothers *in the arcade*
You used to play Super Mario Brothers, *the board game*

His Best Bars:

You look like a bum that's been squatting outside of soup kitchens
Growing up with dreams of joining up with the Fu-Schnickens
Until you found out they weren't Asian
Then you felt like you was mocked, started listening to 'Pac
But all the thugs dissed you, I hit with the power of Shaq so it ain't nothing for me to Chip Fu

An underground staple since the late nineties, Pumpkinhead was worthy of respect. He was also president of the East Coast division of the Grind Time battle league. But the vet choked—meaning, he forgot his lines—both in the second and overtime rounds. That was basically an automatic L. From there, all I had to do was not fuck up. Every age-related punchline landed, and I sealed the win at the end of the third round: *I know the East Coast might not like me after this, but I hope y'all still do / Even though I just murdered your president, John Wilkes Booth.* The warehouse went nuts, and I took the dub. Sadly, PH passed away in 2015, but his contributions to the culture will always be remembered. RIP Robert Alan Diaz.

Date: November 5, 2009

Location: Toronto

Opponent: Kid Twist, a twenty-three-year-old known for his wit and nerdy charm; the biggest battle rapper in Canada

Angle of Attack: Make fun of his geeky demeanor, bird-beak nose, and Asian-fetish vibe

My Best Bars:

Why do they keep setting me up against these f—t kids
'Cause I already battled Illusion-Z and he's just like you, with a Latin twist
I will Kanye this bitch
Hop on stage and shit
And snatch the mic from Taylor Twist
He's infatuated with my people, an Asian culture geek
A petite physique with a vulture's beak
You see, he knows more about Asians than me and Tantrum
He's the one who taught me the Korean anthem
You would fantasize about having slanted eyes
And calls himself "The Last Samurai"

His Best Bars:

It's ironic that you're Asian and you can't make tracks
But all your bright ideas seem dimmer in your lamp shade hats
So dead the drama, Jonnie
The only thing you ever killed was Tamagotchis
You only pull cards in Yu-Gi-Oh!
You only rap raw making sushi rolls
Does anyone else recognize him from his movie role? RUFIO!

Out of all the places in the world, you wouldn't think Canada—friendly, polite Canada—would be a battle-rap capital. But they love the sport like poutine up there, and they breed some savage spitters too. For this headline match, I was paired against the bizarro white Canadian version of me: a skinny, nerdy, razor-sharp MC named Kid Twist. Leading up to it, I was on the Gas Money Millionaires tour—my first North American run—and I was burned out from back-to-back shows and nonstop partying. By the time I landed in Twist's home turf of Toronto, I'd barely memorized my lines. It showed. I was a little sloppy; he was surgical. The hometown crowd was in his corner. No excuses, though—it was close, but chalk this one up for Canada. Years later, Kid Twist went on to become a successful screenwriter and penned the Eminem-produced, Joseph Kahn–directed movie *Bodied*—co-starring yours truly.

Date: February 8, 2015

Location: Toronto

Opponent: Conceited, a twenty-six-year-old Brooklyn gun-talk rapper known for being on Nick Cannon's MTV show *Wild 'n Out*

Angle of Attack: Ambush him with short jokes, fake-thug slander, and *Wild 'n Out* shade

My Best Bars:

There's perks to being short, I don't care what y'all think
When you got small feet, you can get the Jordans all cheap
When you order a shot at the bar, that's a tall drink
He got three hot tubs at the crib, all sinks

His Best Bars:

Why do you use R's instead of L's when you speak?
He be like, "Herro! My favorite rapper is Ril Wayne."
I mean, now that's the truth, I ain't racist
I don't know if that's somethin' you do 'cause you're Asian
But in this battle I'll give you a L so you can use it in your language

I hadn't battled on a big stage in over five years when I got a call from Organik, founder of King of the Dot, Canada's premier battle-rap league. They'd just partnered with Drake—a huge fan—who offered to bankroll an event stacked with all-stars. Around this time, mainstream rappers were paying money to stage battles for their own entertainment, like rap's version of *Squid Game*. Drake even name-dropped me in the press conference as a rapper he looked forward to seeing. They matched me up against Conceited, whose role on *Wild 'n Out* made him one of the most recognizable battle rappers. His style comes from the corner of rap that's more obsessed with guns than a red-blooded Texan—bullets were flying past my head every other line. I fired back with a barrage of snaps about his height and his fake-gangster persona. The result: the most viewed and most debated battle of my career. To this day, fans still argue over who won.

Date: August 21, 2015

Location: Toronto

Opponent: Dizaster, a thirty-year-old Lebanese American from L.A., an absolute psychopath and notorious battle figure

Angle of Attack: Mock his 'roid rage, call him a terrorist, say he has no life outside of battling

My Best Bars:

You made your whole career out of calling yourself a terrorist
Like is anybody scared of him?
Let me give you comparisons of your usual terrorist and delusional American
They throw rocks at tanks, you like rocking tanks
They blew up the New York skyline
You blow up my timeline
They create a hostage situation
You couldn't handle a caustic situation
You're just a spoiled prince of Arabia
Appropriating terrorist culture, Iggy Israelea

His Best Bars:

Congraturations, Ninja Gaiden, your fake fight got millions of page hits
As soon as your shit went viral online, you called up your sensei and told him "Ninja, we made it!"
Ain't no respect and honor for a cat
Who walked around and turned his back
On the same art form that got him where he's at
You figure after all the acupuncture, you'd have a spinal column in your back
But it's probably not attached, 'cause you went to Hollywood to act
And on top of all of that your biggest accomplishment in rap
Is paying to get Waka Fraka on a track

Diz and I came up together as teenagers in the L.A. scene, so by this point we'd already crossed paths plenty. I've never met anyone more obsessed with battle rap than he is—it's admirable when someone fully devotes their life to a highly specific skillset. He's battled so many different types of opponents that he has a full Rolodex of insults, with files labeled "fat," "Black," "Latino," and of course, "Asian." His Asian folder was stacked—he even had some leftover bars from a canceled battle with Jin. Diz's ethnic insults hit harder because he struck an imposing figure—stocky and tatted up, with a face locked in a perma-snarl. In his early days, that ultra-aggressive demeanor and delivery intimidated the opposition. He actually seemed like he had legit anger issues. (The year prior, Diz famously punched Math Hoffa in the middle of a heated battle.) But since then, he added more humor to his arsenal—some of which, he later told me, I had influenced.

The Dizaster I faced in this battle was ready to use some of my own comedic tactics against me—but to an extreme that I wasn't expecting. Thirty minutes before our battle, nobody could find him. When they finally announced his name, he reappeared completely bald, dressed in Buddhist monk robes, and mock-bowed to me. Like I said: absolute psychopath.

Date: February 25, 2023

Location: Toronto

Opponent: Rone, a thirty-four-year-old white bro from Philly and Barstool Sports personality

Angle of Attack: Paint him as a MAGA frat boy

My Best Bars:

When we were yellin' "Black Lives Matter," tryin' to stop Asian hate
You were storming the Capitol tryin' to keep Caucasians safe
In Ferguson, you thought the cops saved the day

With Breonna Taylor, you would not say her name
You were mad as shit at Kaepernick, you little sports boy
You won't take one knee for George Floyd, but I bet you'd take two knees for Dave Portnoy

His Best Bars:

Some kung fu put Bong Joon-ho through the linoleum
You had three Anderson .Paak beats and you still couldn't blow with him
Now he's at MSG and this pussy's throwin' sodium

But it's gettin' hard to tell what kind of accent he's flexin'
You got a weird twang like a Cantonese Texan
I'll leave you crying in H Mart like Japanese Breakfast
I got the smoke, like fajitas in your Applebee's section

I was long retired from battle rap when tragedy pulled me back. My friend Pat Stay, one of the GOATs, was shockingly killed in an altercation near his hometown in Nova Scotia. Our community rallied for a memorial fundraiser, bringing legends out of hiatus—the likes of Hollow Da Don, Dizaster, The Saurus, and Jin. My opponent was Rone, who came across like a regular-degular, goofy white bro from Pennsylvania. Beneath the surface, though, Rone was deceptively clever. Case in point: In the middle of our battle, he dropped *I'll leave you crying in H Mart like Japanese Breakfast*—referencing the title of Michelle Zauner's memoir. That was such a deep Asian American cut that it caught me by surprise and probably went over the heads of the audience. We've come a long way from dog-eating jokes. The event ended up raising over $200,000 for Pat's family. RIP Pat Stay.

Believe it or not, at the end of each battle—after spewing offensive shit back and forth with my opponent for an hour or two—we'd always shake hands like MMA fighters who put it all on the line in the spirit of competition. Every match was like my own Netflix stand-up special, and I wanted each to stand on its own as a classic. All of them added to the catalog, leaving me with a mix of scars and stripes, ready for whatever the world was going to throw at me.

CHAPTER EIGHT

KTOWN WAS A RIOT

When I was nineteen, on the last leg of my first rap tour, I got my first tattoo: KOREATOWN, in giant Old English script spread across my chest. I wanted it bold and aggressive, and the artist delivered. Still, I avoided water parks for a couple of years after one too many mean mugs from Mexican gangsters. The V-necks and tank tops I preferred didn't help either—when I wore them, all you could see were the middle three letters: EAT. It was like my bird chest was begging for food.

The tattoo itself was an easy choice. At the time, I couldn't think of anything else I wanted permanently inked on my body to represent me. You see, I'm Korean, and I'm Korean American—but more than either, I'm *Koreatown*. Of all those categories, I identify with Koreatown the most. After all, a neighborhood as insular yet sprawling as Ktown is its own ecosystem—it's damn near its own country. There's also a long tradition of rappers identifying themselves through their hometowns, from N.W.A's "Straight Outta Compton" to Nas's "NY State of Mind" to OutKast's "ATLiens." These works create new, previously untold narratives of their neighborhoods. Though other parts of L.A. helped raise me—skating in Pico-Union, rapping in South Central, partying in Silver Lake and Hollywood—my roots have always been firmly planted in Koreatown. I've lived here basically my whole life, for better and for worse.

Some basic facts: Los Angeles is home to the largest Korean population outside of Korea, and Koreatown has the highest concentration. After the 1965 Immigration Act, a wave of Koreans moved to the roughly 2.7-square-mile neighborhood west of downtown and established businesses. Before we were crying in H Mart, we were buying in Olympic Market, the first Korean-owned grocery in L.A. It was opened in 1971 by entrepreneur Hi Duk Lee, who laid the foundation of modern Ktown. In 1980, Lee worked with the L.A. City Council to have Ktown officially recognized as a neighborhood; two years later, the first Koreatown street signs were erected. And in 1989, at age three, I moved in—and never left.

You might say my investment in the hood has paid off. In the aftermath of the '92 riots, Koreatown—much like my household—felt tense and volatile, a community locked in a defensive stance. But as I came of age, so too did the neighborhood, which now packs more people into every block than anywhere else in L.A. With the rise of K-culture, what I once saw as just the part of town I grew up in became a hot spot for food and nightlife—maybe *too* hot. (I'll probably find true love in Ktown before I find a parking spot.) As my rap career grew, I helped boost Koreatown's profile by repping it proudly. In return, I benefited from the Korean wave, because Korea's rising brand suddenly made Ktown cool. The gun-toting shop owners protecting 5th and Western back in 1992 could never have imagined that twenty-five years later, legions of foreigners would invade those same blocks to buy tteokbokki and BTS keychains. My neighborhood, and my chest, was getting gentrified.

If Ktown had never blown up, I might've left. Like most teenagers, I had the urge to escape my hometown. Then I went on my first tour and visited dozens of random cities across the country. I got a glimpse of a different kind of Asian American experience, where being the token Asian was a burden. Those kids would tell me how shocked they were to see someone like me on stage: a bold, unapologetic Asian American. It made me realize how lucky I was to be from Ktown, a place where kimchi-squatting toughs chain-smoked Parliaments in strip mall parking lots, daring you to look twice. It's where being Korean is a badge of honor, a source of confidence. When I got my KOREATOWN tattoo at the end of that tour, it was with a renewed sense of pride in where I came from. The truth is, I never wanted to leave—and maybe I couldn't. It was all too easy to coast as the hometown hero where "Dumbfoundead" became synonymous with Koreatown. Skipping security lines at every club, getting free drinks, hooking up with girls who already knew who I was . . . who wouldn't enjoy life as the local golden boy? I got stuck in that man-about-Ktown persona, spending countless nights in my twenties getting wasted at the same neighborhood haunts. Ktown enabled me, and I took full advantage.

Now that I'm older, I'm proud that Ktown is a big part of who I am. The three F's have kept me around: family, food, and FOBs. My mom still lives there, and I have to look after her—good Asian children never put their parents in retirement homes (although it would make my life *so* much easier). As far as restaurants, I've heard actual Koreans claim that the food in Koreatown is better than in Seoul. And Korean culture and people remain a source of comfort. It's a place to ground me, regardless of where my career takes me. I go out into the world equipped with everything the neighborhood taught me.

All that said, I'm having that KOREATOWN tattoo removed—not due to gentrification or because I'm turning my back on my hometown, but because it's become a hindrance to my acting career. Who knows, I might want to play a Japanese or Chinese dude someday. Besides, I don't need it written across my chest to rep Ktown till the day I die. It's in my DNA.

And if you've spent nearly four decades in one neighborhood like I have, every block, every strip mall, and every alley has a story attached to it. So, here's my personal history of Koreatown, told through the places that made me who I am.

Building Blocks

Growing up, I lived in three different apartments in Ktown, each on a different street.

Mariposa Avenue (ages 3–8)

The word "mariposa" means butterfly in Spanish, a beautiful symbol of transformation and freedom. For me, though, Mariposa conjures up the image of a dingy one-bedroom apartment in a building with a sweatshop in the basement, where Univision played on a nonstop loop. My mom worked odd jobs in that basement, and even as a preschooler I would help out. At the time, I spoke only Korean and Spanish. One of the first movies I remember watching was the horror flick *Child's Play* in Spanish. If you think Chucky was scary in English, try watching that shit in Spanish. I heard "¡Hola, me llamo Chucky!" in my nightmares.

Harvard Boulevard (ages 8–13)

Three blocks away from my family's Harvard apartment was Oxford Avenue, so I grew up constantly hearing the names of two elite universities. Wishful thinking for a miscreant like me, but they sounded better than Dropout Street and Stoner Lane. My crew back then was like an L.A. version of the movie *Kids*—different ages, different ethnicities, but the same problems at home. There was Bank, a Thai kid who wore big cubic zirconia earrings and rocked all the illest brands: Akademiks, Pelle Pelle, Eckō, and Phat Farm. I'd buy his hand-me-downs, no matter that they were three sizes too big. Then there was Gavin Snow—his real name—a Native American troublemaker who was equal parts bully and buddy. Rounding out the group was Mikey, a mixed Korean-and-white redhead—like the kid from the movie *Problem Child*—who was four years younger than the rest of us, but the most feral of us all. His dad, a white guy who was never around, let Mikey run wild just like most of our parents did. We had the freedom to wreak havoc like the Bad News Bears of Ktown—a wild, diverse crew doing dumb shit. If we weren't on shoplifting runs, we'd sneak into apartment complexes and swim in their pools until we got kicked out. We'd comb apartment parking garages for unlocked cars to ransack. Mikey, being the baby of the crew, would get sent on the most missions. Sadly, he's been in and out of jail since he was young.

Vermont Avenue (ages 13+)

After my parents split, I moved with my mom and sister to a two-bedroom apartment on Vermont. By then, I considered myself Korean trash—the kimchi-stained version of trailer trash. My youthful shenanigans turned into more serious teenage fuckery, masked by playful names. Laundry Shopping was when we'd sneak into the laundry rooms of random apartment buildings and raid the washers and dryers, running out of buildings clutching wet clothes. Pizza Party was when we'd order pizzas to a random address, wait for the delivery guy to arrive and exit his vehicle, and then sneak into his car to steal the remaining pizzas from his route. And Demolition Derby was what we'd play in the stolen Honda Civics—unlocked using a master key—that we'd joyride into Griffith Park. Scumbag behavior, all of it, especially because our targets were working-class locals. We were teens without guidance, jumping from adventure to adventure, with no plan for the future.

I might've walked a straighter path if I had hung out with more church Koreans. But even though I spent my whole childhood in Ktown, my only real connection to other Korean kids was through the Hong family, who lived across the street from us on Harvard. Their son, Andy, and daughter, Mimi, were the same age as me and my sister, and we became tight. Otherwise, I never associated with the church crowd or the main Ktown crews, and I drifted even further from them in my later years. I avoided the gangster types who adopted the full AZN look: crispy white tees, K-Swiss sneakers, and spiky hair atop skin fades. Maybe it's more accurate to say they avoided me. They always thought I was a weirdo. Even when I started rapping, they said my rap style was too nerdy: "I ain't trying to hear those space raps. Play that Mack 10!" Those dudes were Ktown cool, and I was in a different galaxy.

Gaju Market

One of my most vivid childhood memories is from the spring of '92. I was six years old, sitting in the backseat of my dad's lemon-yellow Oldsmobile. We were making a family grocery run to Gaju Market, later known as California Market. As we pulled into the parking lot, a frantic security guard hurried to my dad's window, waving his arms. "Get the hell out of here," he yelled in Korean. "The mob is on its way down Western Avenue!"

Mob? What mob? As my dad reversed course, I peered outside the window and saw a crowd of angry people descending Western. My parents had no clue what was going on. They weren't tapped into the Rodney King trial, let alone the fact that the acquittal of four white LAPD officers had just set off chaos in the city. We got home and turned on the news. Luckily, my parents worked downtown, and their stores were left unscathed. The so-called "rooftop Koreans," many of whom had survived war in Korea and had military training, protected some of the area around Gaju. But plenty of other Ktown businesses were looted and burned in the riots, and residents were left to fend for themselves. I watched it unfold on TV for the next week, oblivious to the larger context or the effect it was having on the people in my neighborhood. As a kid, I remember thinking that the looting actually looked kinda fun. Shoot, we needed a new TV too.

When I got older, I learned what 1992 really was: the moment when the long-simmering tension between Korean shop owners and the Black and Latino communities reached a boiling point. In March of '91, just weeks before the Rodney King beating, fifteen-year-old Latasha Harlins, a Black high school student, was shot and killed in South L.A. by a Korean store owner, Soon Ja Du, over a $1.79 bottle of orange juice. Soon after came Ice Cube's track "Black Korea," where he snarled, *So pay respect to the Black fist / Or we'll burn your store right down to a crisp.* And then, of course, came Sa-i-gu—what Koreans call 4/29—the date the L.A. uprising began.

From my own life, I could understand pieces of both sides. There was truth to the perception that Koreans had profited from liquor stores and beauty shops in the hood without giving much back. But then I'd hear my dad and his friends talk about the abuse they took, and I could see how immigrants grinding it out on foreign soil could cling to their own prejudices too. Their views were largely shaped by the random unruly customer or the alarmist stories they saw on the news. And because many Korean immigrants didn't speak much English, there was almost no real dialogue between the communities. Without dialogue, empathy is hard to come by. So, imagine my father's disappointment when his teenage son started immersing himself in Black culture. I was already hooked, but his disapproval probably pushed me toward it even more.

In my midtwenties, I got a tattoo on my left arm of a hand holding a Molotov cocktail with *'92* on it. Next to it is Rodney King's famous plea in all caps: CAN WE ALL GET ALONG?

Hopefully, we can. That's part of the legacy of being raised in the Ktown of my era—the trauma, and the lessons, of life after '92. For a Korean kid like me, raised on Black culture, it meant something to help bridge that divide.

Shatto Park

Not all my Ktown lessons were so political. The first time I smoked weed was in the public park at Shatto Recreation Center, off 4th Street and Westmoreland Avenue. Shatto was a central spot for Ktown kids to hoop and hang out; after dark, it wasn't a place to linger. I was in seventh grade when my Mexican homie Lucas and I scored a dime bag from a classmate. We headed to Shatto after school to smoke it. Lucas broke up a Swisher Sweet, dumped the guts, filled it with stress—for you Gen-Z stoners spoiled on dispensaries, that's weed with stems and seeds—and rolled it carefully into a blunt. You know in movies, when an underage kid smokes for the first time and immediately breaks into a coughing fit? Well, not only did I do that, but I almost threw up the Hot Cheetos I'd just eaten. Still, I fought through it. Afterward, Lucas and I shared a Black & Mild, a popular hood cigar we'd seen older heads use as a post-blunt dessert. Pretty soon, all my clothes smelled like Black & Milds. By the time I got to high school, I was a budding pothead—pun intended.

KIWA

The Koreatown Immigrant Workers Alliance (KIWA) is an activist group that fights for fair wages and labor rights for immigrant workers in L.A. When I was in high school, I started going to their tiny office once a week—not because I had any special interest in immigration rights, but because that was where Jeet Kune Flow was held every Sunday. It was an open-mic freestyle session started by a radical Asian American promoter and activist named Kublai Kwon. Kublai wanted to create an arena for Asian Americans to freestyle, since most Asian kids who liked hip-hop were too shy to rap in public. I wasn't like that—I had Black and Latino friends who egged me on—but there were definitely Korean kids from the neighborhood who needed a safe space to practice. It was ironic: The Korean rappers who came to Jeet Kune Flow looked the part—like clones of Snoop Dogg and Kurupt—but their freestyles were predictable. I, on the other hand, resembled a meek incel, but I could rap circles around everybody. In fact, Jeet Kune Flow was the least intimidating of the open mics I frequented. Project Blowed had turned me into a freestyle animal. If Jeet Kune Flow was like doing stand-up at a dive bar, Blowed was *Def Comedy Jam*—a huge step up.

Even though the competition at Jeet Kune Flow wasn't as fierce, it was still a valuable experience. I got the opportunity to rhyme with my Asian American peers—and no matter the skill level, freestyling was a necessary outlet for all of us. Week after week, being in that room pushed everyone to get better.

A final note on immigration rights: Even though my only experience at KIWA was to freestyle in their space, I did end up performing at La Gran Marcha on March 25, 2006, the massive immigration reform protest in downtown L.A. that was, at the time, considered the largest public protest in US history. ¡Sí, se puede!

Café Bleu

In 2018, I released a six-song EP named after my favorite Ktown bar: *Café Bleu*. On the title track, I paid tribute to the place where I drank away so many nights.

Neon lights and velvet couches like a casting call
The glasses clinking and the whispers from the bathroom stalls
Half a block from Chapman Plaza, come and sip with squad
It's a painful, lonely, small world after all

Since before I could legally drink, Café Bleu has been like the Cheers bar for Ktown barflies. The bar first opened its doors in 2001, wedged into the corner of an anonymous strip mall that's also home to a 7-Eleven and a few popular Korean restaurants. People waiting in line for tables often peek in as Bleu's smoke-breakers head back to their drinks. And it's not exactly an inviting place. From the outside, it looks like a dimly lit dungeon.

But inside, Bleu felt like a second home. I can't remember my first time there, but it looks pretty much the same now as it did then. The owner, James, has always shown me mad love. It's been my pregame and end-of-the-night stop for most of my rap career, from the early days when I had to budget my drinks, to my thirties, when I'd buy a bottle just because it was Tuesday. I've spent so much money at Bleu, I must've put waitresses through college. I've also done a lot of coke in the bathroom (sometimes we'd playfully call the place Café Blow)—hopefully sending some of my plugs to college too. Bleu became part of my personality during the era when I embraced the lifestyle of a full-time Ktown party animal.

What made Bleu special went beyond the booze. Like any classic neighborhood dive, it was a place for locals to connect—specifically, a refuge for Asian entertainers to commiserate and sometimes perform. Far East Movement had their first show at Bleu; Bobby Lee did stand-up on the bar's modest stage. Back in the day, I was a rookie with a front-row seat to a league of older artists who'd spent years trying to

"Ktown Was a Riot"
Artwork by Aaron Kai

3RD ST.
한밭설렁탕
HANBAT SHUL -LUNG-TANG
가주마켙
CALIFORNIA MARKET
café
bleu
DICK'S
LIQUOR
노래방
KARAOKE
주류완비

BEVERLY BLVD.

NORMANDIE AVE.
BOWL
FULL BAR
SHATTO
39
LANES
Black & Mild

make it in the industry. Before *Crazy Rich Asians* cracked Hollywood wide open, Bleu regulars included people like Daniel Dae Kim, Ken Jeong, and C. S. Lee. They'd swap audition horror stories, the kind I became familiar with once I started dabbling in acting. Like the time a bunch of us were up for a role on the CBS sitcom *2 Broke Girls.* The waiting room was stacked with Asian American heavyweights like Sung Kang and Justin Chon. We'd all prepped the script they sent, but when the casting agent came out, he flipped it: "Hey everyone, we want you to try these lines in an Asian accent." Everybody groaned. Sung tried to play the voice of reason, saying the best way to get revenge would be to book the role and bring it up directly with the director. But Justin wasn't having it—he ripped up the sheets and stormed out. Later, he wrote an NBCNews.com op-ed that went viral: "I Walked Out on a Racist Audition." Meanwhile, I stayed. I put on the accent—which I sucked at—and didn't even get a callback. I felt like a sellout but started to understand why the Bleu OGs could get so bitter.

Not every conversation at Bleu was that heavy. Just as often, a spontaneous round of shots could spark a lively debate about someone's half-baked script idea. In typical L.A. fashion, even the staff had Hollywood dreams. Pedro, the buff bartender and aspiring actor, often joined the chorus of complaints about how he wasn't getting cast either.

On the flip side, Bleu was also where we'd take visiting stars from Korea, because even the biggest overseas names could get lit there undisturbed. No randos, no superfans, no paparazzi—just Bong Joon-ho or Lee Byung-hun downing whiskey on a random weeknight like everyone else.

These days, Bleu is one of the few places that feels like the old

Ktown—the one that stood defiantly together after the riots, not the one with a new boba shop on every corner. I rarely go to Bleu now; I drink less and value my sleep more. The outro on the *Café Bleu* EP is about leaving the bar and finally heading home, like walking out of purgatory. But Bleu will always be more than just a bar—it was a place where comrades on the come-up gathered to wind down and figure things out together, without judgment.

Misery loves company, I love my friends to death
Everything is everything when you have nothing left
Lovers become enemies and leave you with the check
Where everybody knows your name when everyone else forgets . . .

Beverly & Reno

There's a scene in the 1997 film *Boogie Nights* in which porn star Dirk Diggler gets picked up by a random guy in a truck and driven to an abandoned parking lot. He offers Dirk money to watch him jerk off; he's fascinated by Dirk's endowment, even if he insists he's "not gay." Reluctantly, Dirk pulls out his missile and starts stroking it. The scene ends when the truck guy's friends pull up out of nowhere and kick the shit out of the star. But that's not the part I related to. It's the idea of having this one freakish talent that strangers obsessed over. Freestyling was my twelve-inch dick.

When I was twenty, I was roommates with a mixed-race Black-white kid named Sahtyre, a partner in rhyme and petty crime. A couple years my junior, Sahtyre was a damn near prodigy. He was my closest friend in the scene and an unusual guy. He spoke like a hood dude from Venice Beach or a surfer from the streets. Like me, Sahtyre came from a tough upbringing. Actually, his was more fucked up—his mom was addicted to crack. Living without generational wealth was a challenge, but generational poverty could be a breaking point. My Latino homies' parents worked way worse jobs than mine. I once went to a Mexican friend's house and saw a dozen people living in a two-bedroom. Even at my lowest point, it wasn't as bad as some of the other families I saw around me. Seeing their struggle kept me grounded while also making me cognizant of the privilege I had as an Asian American.

Around 2006, Sahtyre and I were barely making ends meet but having the time of our lives as two of the best freestyle rappers in the city. We both had addictive personalities. Through the party scene, we got to know a rich white dude from the Westside named Wes. Not unlike a lot of rich white dudes from there, he was into streetwear and trying to get his hat company off the ground. Also not unlike a lot of rich white dudes from the Westside, Wes had easy access to coke. So, he would come over to our apartment with blow, just to watch us cypher. When we let him inside, he'd hold up a baggie, grinning like, "Look what I got!" As we put on beats and started rhyming, Wes would pull out a plate and chop the powder into lines. We'd alternate between rapping and snorting for hours. I could tell Wes was thrilled by every punchline, gasping "Oh, shit!" at every other bar, almost turned on by the performance. But he wasn't a scumbag; he was genuinely mesmerized by the wordplay. I soaked up that feeling of captivating someone with words they'd never heard strung together. It had been the same at the high school cafeteria. That was the whole point: to blow people's minds with whatever you came up with on the spot. For a time, Wes was like our Don King when we went out.

If other people were cyphering, he'd look at them with disdain and mutter, "Look at these motherfuckers." They weren't dope enough to get free cocaine from him, that's for sure.

Sahtyre and I were becoming famous in party circles all around the city. It helped that we made a memorable pair—a funny Black-and-Asian duo, straight out of *Rush Hour.* We could go anywhere and get props. One night, we'd impress a bunch of girls at a fashion event or rhyme at a hipster party in Silver Lake; the next, we'd hit a Mexican backyard function in South Gate or an all-Black rap party and kill it there too. Of course, we were always prepared to battle, and as two skinny, ratty-looking rappers—Sahtyre would often get called the kid from *Holes*—there was no shortage of challengers. We got so good at tag-teaming that we eventually entered official two-man battles together.

So, there I was: living terribly, making basically no money, but roaming around the city like a top dog, feeding off the *oohs* and *aahs* from unknown girls, intoxicated from the free drinks and blunts that were our party favors. I'd return home to a tiny apartment, lay my head down on a grimy pillow on a foldout couch, and feel like a king. I had found my calling in a weird little subculture and went all in, whether or not there was a future—or fortune—in it. It reminds me now of the cheerleaders in the Netflix documentary *Cheer.* They spend every waking moment practicing and perfecting a very specific craft, all the while knowing they're never going to get rich off that talent. Likewise, my life was consumed with freestyle rap and battling, even if I couldn't imagine how to make a viable career out of it. Little did I know, my party trick was about to give my life real shape for the first time.

A Parking Lot by the Wiltern

My "hometown hero" pass gave me carte blanche at places like Bleu. In my early twenties, I was feeling myself a little too much—but I wasn't immune to getting checked. I learned that the hard way. One drunken night when I was twenty-four, I flirted with a girl at a bar, and we exchanged numbers—no biggie. I got home and shot her a couple playful texts and forgot all about it. A few days later, an unknown number started hitting me with cryptic messages. They would've been easy to ignore, except the sender was dropping personal info: where I lived, my sister's name, even where my mom worked. No direct threats, but unsettling nonetheless, because I had no idea who was sending them.

After this went on for a week or so, I felt like the prisoner in *Oldboy,* scrambling to figure out whom I'd wronged, and how.

I called the number. "Yo, who are you, bro?"

A husky male voice answered, "Meet me on the third floor of the parking garage on Wilshire and Western tonight at ten p.m." He paused. "Come alone or *I'll fuck your shit up.*"

Well damn. The situation seemed sketchy at best, yet curiosity (and pride) compelled me to find out why I was being targeted. So, I drove to the garage, but not before calling a homie to stand by in case shit got hairy and I needed emergency backup.

At Wilshire and Western, I parked on the third floor and got out of my car. A guy in a Lakers jersey stepped out of a white SUV, phone in hand. He was still texting me as he approached. I didn't recognize him but could immediately tell he was Chinese or Vietnamese and not Korean—which made the situation scarier. Finally, we met face to face.

"You're texting my girl," he said.

I was confused for a second—there were probably fifteen open convos with different girls on my phone—but the psychotic look in his eyes turned my memory jog into a sprint. *Oh shit . . . bar girl.*

Instantly, my mouth started damage control. "Bro, I didn't know she had a dude. I would never overstep. Much respect."

I kept dropping the keyword "respect" like a spell. It didn't work. He went back to his car, grabbed a gun, and came back and pressed it to my temple.

"Apologize," he demanded.

I spit out a million sorrys, shitting bricks, all while he filmed me with his phone. Not only did this fool want to punk me, he wanted to keep the footage for posterity.

Then, my gift of gab kicked in. I stopped defending myself and started placating his ego, telling him that I'd be mad too, but this situation wasn't worth the stress. He eventually admitted that she'd broken up with him weeks ago, and he was "going through it." Sensing a new angle, I leaned in and counseled him about how to get over an ex. Just minutes earlier, I thought I was gonna get pistol-whipped.

Now, he was saying, "My bad, bro. I'm overreacting."

I replied, "Nah, it's all good—let's grab a drink at Bleu sometime," knowing damn well I never wanted to see him again in my life.

We dapped up, and I drove away, almost teary-eyed. I realized in that moment that I'd made a mistake by hitting on the wrong girl—but beyond that, it opened my eyes to the dudes in my hood who didn't give a fuck about local clout. *Look at this soft motherfucker thinking he's the shit because he raps,* I imagined them thinking. It pissed them off even more that a broke nerd was trying to steal their girl.

There's a scene in the movie *Slam* where the spoken-word poet Saul Williams, surrounded by a mob of inmates about to beat him down in a prison yard, suddenly starts spitting poetry until they back off. He disarms them with his words. That scene stuck with me, because all my life I talked myself out of trouble, just like in that parking garage. But my manager Brian Lee warned me that my mouth wouldn't always save me. He convinced me that I needed to get out of the craze of Ktown, so I moved to Culver City, into the same building he lived in. It was the most productive—and most boring—stretch of my twenties. When I couldn't bear the quiet, I snuck back to Ktown to party. One year later, I moved back home for good.

The LINE L.A.

We had our go-to bar, but we needed our go-to club. And not the "booking" clubs of Ktown yore, where groups of hard-drinking guys sat at tables with bottles of Chivas and fruit plates, calling on waiters to bring whichever girls caught their eye.

The Ktown scene was changing: New spots popped up, and the neighborhood was becoming something bigger than the one I grew up in. By the mid-2010s, gentrification had already crept in, but the opening of the LINE L.A. Hotel on Wilshire and Normandie was the clearest sign the neighborhood was turning. Once a rundown building called the Wilshire Plaza Hotel, the twelve-story tower was completely transformed into an IG-friendly hipster haven. When it reopened as the LINE L.A. in 2014, it felt like Ktown was officially on the map as a tourist destination. The *New York Times* even declared that "its biggest accomplishment is introducing visitors to the gems of little-known Koreatown," as if we were some best-kept secret.

The thing about gentrification in Ktown is that the culture didn't get pushed out—it got packaged and sold. The Koreanness itself was the draw. So, the developers behind the LINE knew exactly what they were doing. From the start, they pitched it as "the first lifestyle hotel in the United States to draw upon Korean and Korean American culture, food, and design." That meant tapping in with actual Ktown people—starting with L.A.'s most famous Korean American chef, Roy Choi, to open the hotel's two restaurants, Pot and Commissary.

A quick word on Roy: He pioneered the modern food-truck scene in 2008 with Kogi and his twist on Korean-Mexican fusion. In the early days of my career, Roy would come to my shows with burritos stashed in his jacket to feed the starving rappers backstage. Aside from giving me free food, he was a genuinely supportive hyung who looked out for me—which means a lot, because he's basically Korean American royalty. Like me, Roy shares a deep love for the mix of cultures in L.A. With our longtime ties to the Latino community, we might be two of the most Latino Koreans in the city.

Roy is also a serious hip-hop head. As he got his two spots off the ground at LINE, he wanted to inject more of a nightlife energy into the place. There was no club on-site, but the huge lobby—an open space surrounded by banquettes, with a full bar area in the rear—had potential. By day, it was all coffee sippers and laptop warriors; by night, it was crickets. Roy pitched DJ Zo and me on throwing a weekend party there and inviting our friends. Little did we know that the LINE lobby would soon become the hottest Asian nightlife spot in Southern California.

Right time, right place, right people. Ktown was enjoying its crossover moment, but most nightclubs still catered to old-timers who wanted bottle-and-fruit waiter service, girls ushered to their table, and EDM instead of rap. Locals like me and college kids who grew up on hip-hop weren't trying to dress up for that on a Friday night. The LINE offered something totally different: a weekend soundtrack of peak Kanye, Drake, Future, and YG, all in the heart of Ktown. With Zo as resident DJ, Roy's name adding credibility, and yours truly as de facto host, we were attracting lines around the block in no time, full of young Asian kids dying to turn up. Once inside the lobby, they'd see Zo spinning records up on a platform; I'd often be beside him, hyping up the crowd. As the night wore on—and the bottles kept flowing—girls would climb up and twerk. The vibe was like the best house party you've ever been to, with some of the baddest ABGs (Asian Baby Girls) you've ever seen. The turntable setup was notoriously janky and so was the sound system, sometimes forcing Zo to bring his own speakers. But house parties aren't raking in $30,000 at the bar. The party was doing so well that the LINE kept it going for years, even though I'm sure they fielded a noise complaint or two. I can only imagine a couple from Ohio heading to their room and walking straight into three hundred Asians getting ratchet in the lobby.

For a long, blurry stretch of the mid- to late 2010s, our weekend ritual was to pregame at Bleu and then head straight to the LINE. It got so big that Snoop Dogg pulled up once with his Korean American manager, Ted Chung. Zo met Solange in the LINE lobby and later ended up doing events with her. It was like our own little Studio 54, right in the middle of my stomping grounds.

The best part of all was the convenience—I lived seven blocks away. When last call hit at around 1:45 a.m., we'd round up some ladies and walk back to my apartment, stopping at CVS to stock up on booze. The afterparties lasted until sunrise, pissing off my roommate Jaysn to no end.

By 2018, the LINE weekend party had run its course, as all events eventually do. What a time. I'd like to think a few years of Asians turning up might've even slowed the gentrification down.

Park's BBQ

It wasn't until I turned thirty that I truly felt appreciated in my hometown. Sure, every bartender and bouncer from Western to Vermont knew my face, but there was a specific recognition that eluded me. Let me explain.

In 2003, Park's BBQ opened in a shopping plaza on the corner of Olympic and Vermont. It wasn't the first Korean barbecue joint in Ktown, and far from the last, but over the years it's earned its Michelin-recommended rep as the city's standard-bearer for prime galbi. By the way, I always thought "L.A." galbi—bone-in, thinly sliced beef short ribs—got its name from Los Angeles, but others swear that it stands for "lateral axis," the way the beef is cut. I'm still claiming this one for L.A.

I first went to Park's as a teenager, when it was the new BBQ on the block. As the restaurant got more famous, the owners started a photo wall by the entrance, featuring its celebrity diners. Every visit, I'd watch the celeb wall grow—from ten photos to fifty to over a hundred. In the early years, it was mostly populated by Korean stars from abroad—PSY, Song Kang-ho, Jang Dong-gun—along with famous Koreans living in L.A., like Dodgers pitcher Park Chan-ho. Then came Korean American notables like actors John Cho and Ken Jeong. As Park's blew up, non-Koreans like Keanu Reeves and Nicolas Cage were added to the mix.

From the moment I saw the Park's wall, I dreamed of being up there. I even thought about secretly sticking up my own photo, like Banksy at the Tate. By the 2010s—after I'd released a half dozen albums putting Ktown on the map—that dream curdled into a grievance: *What the fuck do I have to do to get on this wall? Wait—Jason Biggs is up there?* Going to Park's started to infuriate me. *C'mon, that Korean Olympic wrestler only won a fucking bronze!* Finally, it became an all-out grudge. *Andy Milonakis? Really?* (He's the homie, but still.) I felt like Buggin Out in *Do the Right Thing*, ranting about the pictures on Sal's Pizzeria's wall, except it was ego, not racial pride, that drove my rage. I could accept being ignored by mainstream America, slow as it was to recognize Asian American celebs. But here, in a Korean restaurant? In my own hood? By my own people? It stung like a diss from a family member.

Finally, in 2016, Park's BBQ acknowledged a local Ktown rapper named Dumbfoundead by putting his picture up on the wall. It felt overdue, but I appreciated it. Plus, I got pretty good real estate, closer to the door. Try to spot me next time you're there, sandwiched between Aziz Ansari and Andy Samberg on one side and Korean actor Gong Hyung-jin on the other.

Catalina Liquor

Park's made me wait forever to get up on their wall. My mural, though? I took matters into my own hands.

When a local legend passes away, the neighborhood shows love by painting their face somewhere you can't miss it. That's why you see Biggie all over Brooklyn and Kobe and Nipsey everywhere around L.A. It's the kind of recognition that I craved while I was still breathing—the respect of my neighborhood, my people. But I didn't always feel that love, so I wrote a song about it. "Murals," the first track off my 2016 album *We Might Die,* was my way of manifesting it: *When I die, I'm a God / Paint me large on the wall.*

For the music video, I wanted to have an artist paint a mural of me in real time. I found the perfect location: Catalina Liquor, on Catalina and 8th, with its iconic old-school sign whose giant red-and-yellow panels were visible from blocks away. My homie Joseph Lee went to work on the wall, painting a headshot of me wearing my trademark black beanie while I rapped for the camera. The store owner loved the mural so much that he kept it up for years after the video shoot. It was a point of pride for me, and free promo, even if it became so famous that some people actually thought I was dead. Whenever I felt underappreciated, I could stroll by the mural to have my ego stroked.

Mural mural on the wall
May this legend never fall

It didn't last forever. Some hater tagged over it, so they buffed it, and the wall went back to being blank. It was bound to happen. But four years is a pretty long run for an untagged mural in L.A. Even though it's gone now—like my chest tat will soon be—the legend of Dumbfoundead in Ktown is harder to erase. I had the mural; I got the Park's celebrity wall . . . maybe one day your kids will be going to Dumbfoundead Elementary School on Western Avenue.

CHAPTER NINE

THE KIMCHI CIRCUIT

Koachella

It's the night of the 2009 Korean Culture Show on the Yale University campus, and I'm shivering my ass off because it's cold as fuck in New Haven, Connecticut, even inside this classroom-turned-concert hall in the middle of April.

I'm backstage, waiting my turn as the headline performer for tonight's show. It's not my first performance at a university under similar circumstances—it's not even my first gig at an Ivy League institution. As a high-school dropout, I guess you could say I found my own way into the college system. I didn't get into Harvard like my mom dreamed—but technically, I got into every Ivy.

A nervous Yale undergrad with a bowl cut sidles up next to me; he's clutching a ukulele and taking deep breaths. Apparently, he's next up to perform, and I bet my life that "Just the Way You Are" by Bruno Mars is on his setlist. Around us, students in hanboks scurry around in preparation, part of the Korean traditional music performance that's inevitably on the bill at one of these concerts. In an adjacent hallway, the local taekwondo club is loudly doing warm-ups and stretches. No wooden board stands a chance against these fools. Farther down the hallway, a pack of Asian econ majors are going through the paces of their hip-hop choreography, completing the transformation from nerds to krumping maniacs. Who knew college is where Asian kids with 4.0 GPAs could blossom into bootleg Jabbawockeez? I silently survey this familiar scene as my DJ, Zo, hands me a plate overflowing with Korean church classics: kimbap, japchae, and bulgogi—delicious, by the way—catered from the only Korean restaurant in a twenty-mile radius. Tonight is Koachella with a *K*—and did I mention I'm the headliner? Though, respectfully, that's not saying much.

From backstage, I peer out into the 365-seat auditorium, which is about two-thirds full. Predictably, it's full of Korean kids with job-interview haircuts who don't look much younger than me—even though the drunk-and-stoned lifestyle has added a few years to my twenty-something face. (There's a pocket of non-Asians here, too, early adopters of the Korean wave.) I scan the room feeling a mixture of envy and disdain. It's a weird feeling. These are the kids my parents used to compare me to: the nerdy, model-minority Koreans. The next generation of doctors and lawyers, the future hedge-fund fuckers and start-up bros. The kids I could never catch up to in school. The ones who were lining up six-figure jobs as teenagers while I jumped from one dead-end gig to another. To them, I was the underachieving misfit they left behind in high school.

And yet . . . oh yeah, tonight *I'm* the main draw. I didn't drop a dime of tuition money, but I'm an invited guest in their hallowed halls. As a matter of fact, these fuckers are paying *me* to perform.

It's finally showtime. DJ Zo heads out first to hit the turntables and hype up the crowd for my entrance. The sound is terrible—it's run by teenage Yale students, not audio professionals, after all—and the mic I'm handed is better suited for a physics professor. But none of that shit matters. I'm killing it, double-timing lyrics, playfully roasting members of the audience, and they're eating up my every word. I know many of these students have never seen an Asian American performer like me on stage before, one who can and will say whatever the fuck he wants and get away with it. Any negative feelings I have toward these kids evaporates. I love knowing that some kid out there might see me getting turnt on stage and realize, *Oh shit—we can do that too.*

Later, as we often do at these college gigs, Zo and I will hit an afterparty at a frat house. I'll freestyle for hours, hit on the girls, drink their cold beers, smoke their weed. I've seen a lot of wild shit running the streets of Koreatown, but these college students are on some different shit. They're inhaling pot out of everything from organic apples to futuristic bongs that look like alien lab equipment. And the beer pong? Never could I have imagined that a silly game played with ping-pong balls and red cups of beer would be taken so seriously. You'd think their student loans were riding on the outcome. I'll soon find that a lot of these Yalies are more confused about their lives than I am. They're switching majors, stressed out about their grades, worried about the job market, scared that their parents are going to cut them off. Compared to them, I'm carefree, living the dream.

My bag for an hour's work? A cool $2,500, plus travel expenses for both me and Zo. I kick a few hundred dollars to Zo and keep the rest. I feel rich.

Next week? I'll be flown out to the University of Chicago. After that, something called the Charlotte Dragon Boat Festival.

This was what I called the "kimchi circuit." During my early twenties, it paid my rent, filled my fridge, and kept me going as a professional rapper. Above all, the kimchi circuit gave me a sense of belonging and identity with my own people.

The Origin of the Kimchi Circuit

You've probably heard of the Chitlin' Circuit, which refers to a network of Black-owned venues across a segregated America, where Black entertainers could safely tour and perform in the years before the Civil Rights Movement. The Chitlin' Circuit helped birth the careers of legends like James Brown and Aretha Franklin—shoot, it damn near birthed rock 'n' roll as we know it. It also created paid gigs for scores of other Black performers who never made it big but were at least able to make a living off their talent. The Chitlin' Circuit, operated and attended mostly by Black people, followed a "for us, by us" mentality.

You probably haven't heard of the more niche Chop Suey Circuit, which, during roughly the same time period as the Chitlin' Circuit, performed a similar function for Asian American entertainers, mostly of Chinese, Japanese, and Filipino descent. From the 1930s to the 1950s, at nightclubs like San Francisco's Forbidden City and New York's China Doll, pioneers like Jack Soo and Dorothy Toy performed in vaudeville acts that showcased Asian talent in a way previously unseen stateside. Unlike the Chitlin' Circuit, the Chop Suey Circuit was geared toward white audiences, and the "Oriental"-themed performances often played on racial stereotypes and caricatures. (For example, there was a routine they called the "Coolie Dance," which

I won't get into.) Thus, by contrast, the Chop Suey Circuit followed a "for them, by us" mentality.

And you definitely haven't heard of the "kimchi circuit" of the 2010s—and I know this because I coined the term myself. Like the Chop Suey Circuit, the kimchi circuit furthered Asian representation in entertainment, except it was driven by the Chitlin' ethos—for Asians, by Asians. (I call it the "kimchi circuit" because a lot of the shows were run by Korean people, but it extended to performers of many other Asian backgrounds.) The kimchi circuit was like a bootleg tour for fledgling Asian talent, who performed for Asian crowds in school auditoriums and cultural festivals that smelled like bulgogi and ambition. If you're an Asian American who attended college from approximately 2008 to 2012, there's a high probability you saw me perform at your school, and there's a decent chance that we hit a blunt together afterward too.

So how did the kimchi circuit begin? Starting around 2008, with YouTube taking off, a new class of Asian celebrities emerged, including myself and early video creators who bypassed gatekeepers to directly reach audiences online. Asian American kids figured out how to navigate new platforms quickly, which is why some of the top early YouTubers had names like KevJumba, NigaHiga, Michelle Phan, and Wong Fu Productions. This coincided with the growth of a young, Internet-savvy Asian American demographic who was increasingly hungry to see versions of themselves in the spotlight. Hollywood wouldn't let us in, but the Internet had no gatekeepers.

Prior to the birth of the kimchi circuit, the scene for live Asian entertainment was pretty grim. Every city with a sizable Asian American population has some kind of annual Asian-themed event, whether it be a Vietnamese heritage day in Houston or a Hmong festival in Minneapolis. Likewise, every university with more than a handful of Asian students has a specific student organization designated for that group, the most prominent being the Korean student organizations across California and in the Northeast United States. Those student-run groups staged yearly concerts and talent shows with money from school funding, member dues, and the occasional bake sale. Before we came along, the talent you'd see at these types of events was uber-traditional stuff like fan dances and karate demonstrations—and, if it was modern, you might see a random singer or some amateur dance troupe. It was the same old, same old every year. How many times can you be entertained by some guy doing kung-fu flips or some student singing their heart out off-key? The community, particularly the younger generation, was getting bored.

With the YouTube wave of the aughts came some fresh talent for hire: Timothy DeLaGhetto, Internet personality; Paul "PK" Kim, stand-up comic; AJ Rafael, singer; JustKiddingFilms, comedians; and me, Dumbfoundead, the rapper who probably made the most kimchi circuit stops of them all. There were other Asian MCs, too, like D-Pryde, Decipher, J-Reyez, and Lil Crazed. We'd all run into each other at places like UPenn, Cal Poly Pomona, or the Khmer New Year parade in Long Beach. Among Asian crowds, we were treated like genuine stars; people wanted to see us, take pictures with us, and even party with us. It was a movement that paved the way identity-driven fandoms operate to this day. And the money was good.

At one point, I felt like the kimchi circuit was the most reliable way to support my passion, but eventually I realized that I had to get off it in order to prolong my career.

Brian the Brain

By the time I joined the kimchi circuit, I was a respected Blowedian and a seasoned battler with bragging rights all across the city. I'd achieved what I thought was fame . . . but soon grasped that local fame didn't equate to money. In the early days, being broke didn't really bother me. I felt like I was on top of the world because I was pursuing my passion and succeeding. Living below the poverty line while getting better at my craft felt pure to me—some starving-artist shit. I romanticized my life like I was a youngin in the South Bronx winning B-boy battles or graf wars in the seventies. Those kids probably felt the same way I did. Like a master. Like a king. But skills by themselves don't pay the bills. At some point, I had to figure out my next move.

Once my battles started to circulate online, people increasingly knew my name. But making the jump from being a battle rapper to a recording artist isn't easy. It's like asking an improv comedian to write and star in a scripted film. It's going from real-time magic for a captive audience to building cohesive work that can stand on its own. In battle rap, your material is aimed at one opponent; in music, it's aimed at the world.

In *8 Mile*, B-Rabbit's goal is to get a record deal; and, of course, the real-life Eminem pulled it off with Dr. Dre and Aftermath. However, a lot of the Blowedians I ran with were just freestylers and battle rappers with regular day jobs. On weekdays, they might drive a bus, flip burgers, or work at a call center; but after they punched out, they'd turn into lyrical superheroes. They didn't aspire to make albums, and it wasn't because they were lazy. Making an album requires forethought, structure, collaborators, investment, and time.

Freestyling only demands an active brain and tongue. And honestly, the jump might be even harder in the other direction—a recording artist trying to step in a battle.

Like a lot of my rapper peers, I was working menial jobs while earning my battle bona fides in my free time. I wasn't thinking at all about recording a real album. When I started getting booked for performances, instead of coming with a prepared set list, I'd just freestyle live on stage. "Everyone hold up what's in your pocket," I'd shout to the crowd. Someone would hold up a lighter, and I'd just go off.

Lost my Bic, so now I need a lighter
Steal yours quick, call me a lighter swiper
Extinguish your flow, the firefighter in your cypher
Gonna need that gas, it's about to be an all-nighter

Freestyling was fun and easy—a party trick that I had honed for years to make friends laugh and impress strangers. But it was also getting a little tiresome, and I knew that my gigs would eventually run out of gas if I didn't have some original songs to perform. I needed an album. Which meant I needed motivation and money.

One thing I did have was a partner. I had successfully stolen DJ Zo from my frenemy Lyricks; when he had to go back to Virginia from L.A., I asked Zo to be my roommate. Zo, who is of Filipino and Italian descent, was the perfect yin to my yang. We imagined ourselves to be a classic MC & DJ duo like CL Smooth & Pete Rock or Fresh Prince & DJ Jazzy Jeff, but really, we were more like Jay and Silent Bob. I was the outgoing, loud one; Zo was quiet. I could be an asshole, but he was super nice—no one ever had a problem with Zo. Although Zo didn't mind being in the background, he was an absolute master at his craft and an incredibly skilled DJ. (I still think he's one of the best in the world.) Most important, he was tech-savvy and knew how to run Pro Tools, the essential music-creation software for DIY artists. I told him, "I need to make an album. Stay with me for a few months and record it with me. That can be your rent." So, Zo moved into my place.

That studio apartment was in a building called the Asbury in MacArthur Park, which is still one of the sketchiest neighborhoods in L.A. The rent was $750 per month, which I was able to scrounge up by winning rap battles, selling a little weed, or pocketing from my sister's stash. (At the time, Nat was dating a Vietnamese guy who taught her how to make money selling bootleg copies of Photoshop and other software.) It was a roach-infested, seven-hundred-square-foot crackhouse of an apartment. The worn-out carpet looked straight out of a Netflix true-crime documentary, with permanent stains dotting its ugly brown maze pattern. I remember giving Zo the grand tour when he first moved in: how to unlock the door, where to throw the trash, and how to get rid of the ramen noodles that inevitably clogged the kitchen sink. (Jam them down the pipe with a chopstick, obviously.) And the sleeping arrangement? Well, it was a studio. Instead of beds, we shared an L-shaped sectional couch to sleep, our heads perilously close to touching each other. (Believe it or not, despite living like this, I was still pulling girls—I sometimes kicked Zo out to the lobby of the apartment if I brought one home. Ah, the power of rapping.) Our living conditions got even dicier once I bought a secondhand silk-screen machine so I could print my own merch. Chemical fumes overwhelmed the cramped apartment, to the point where we were both waking up with bloodshot eyes.

But Zo and I weren't complaining. We were hungry artists who were willing to grind to achieve a common goal. We survived on weed, 99-cent Carl's Jr. spicy chicken sandwiches, and five-dollar Hot-N-Ready pizzas from Little Caesars, plus the heady dreams of aspiring musicians. We created music out of love but also out of necessity and survival. We didn't even really know what we were doing. I recorded my vocals in a makeshift booth inside the closet. Zo engineered the tracks from his laptop and added scratches on his turntable setup. That's how we made my first album, *Fun with Dumb*. It was written from the perspective of a young, slightly nerdy, imaginative storyteller who rapped about being cockblocked and getting blue balls. Hey, at least I was being honest.

One of the few songs on *Fun with Dumb* that wasn't about juvenile sex shenanigans was called "Bullets of Truth," one of those lyrical-miracle anthems full of conscious bars that backpackers love.

We have a gang of questions that haven't been answered yet
Why we slangin' weapons to our terrorist threats?
In the last election we ain't know where our votes went
Since the last depression we haven't had this much debt
While the gas investors are only seeing success

I must've written those bars with a tinfoil hat on. I can smell the incense as I read them now.

The music video for "Bullets of Truth"—the first video I ever uploaded to my YouTube channel—was directed by my old sparring partner Lyricks. (Multitalented guy, that Rick.) We shot it on the Asbury rooftop in early 2009 as a teaser for *Fun with Dumb*. But shooting the video wasn't the most significant moment of that winter day. Because that was the day I first met Brian Lee.

I was introduced to Brian by our mutual friend Jennifer Lee, aka TOKiMONSTA, who was then an up-and-coming Korean American music producer. She had attended UC Irvine with him. At the time, Toki and I were just figuring out what our music careers would look like—if you could even call them "careers" then. (Years later, Toki became the first Asian American woman to be nominated in the Best Dance/Electronic Album category at the Grammys, so in retrospect it was smart to take her advice.) If you wanted to be a professional musician, Toki told me, you had to have a press kit with professional photos. And since Brian happened to be a hobbyist photographer, she said he would shoot mine for free to build up his portfolio.

Brian was studying for the LSAT at the time, and he later told me a story that reveals exactly how his brain is wired. Back then, the test was on Scantrons—you had to fill in bubbles with a No. 2 pencil. Most people showed up with five freshly sharpened pencils. But Brian had read a study that said every minute saved on a standardized test could raise your score by two points. Since sharp tips catch on the paper, he came armed with five *dull* pencils. He calculated that he could save one second per bubble—across 180 questions, that added up to three full minutes, which could be the difference between a state school and the Ivy League. That was Brian in a nutshell: an obsessive optimizer who had a hack for everything.

So, Brian pulled up to the Asbury to take my picture before the "Bullets of Truth" video shoot. Turns out his divorced dad lived in the MacArthur Park area, so he was already familiar with the hood. Though only five years my elder and still in his twenties, Brian immediately struck me as an extremely talkative, inquisitive, slightly annoying older uncle—he was like the Korean Gary Vee. Toki had shown Brian videos of my battles, and he was impressed. He excitedly told me that he saw my talent straight away and was especially taken aback by how fluently I was able to navigate the world of hip-hop as a fellow Korean American. Brian was on track to attend law school but harbored start-up ambitions after a stint in Silicon Valley. That experience infected him with tech-bro enthusiasm. His brain was primed on total addressable markets, ownership, and growth hacks. Meanwhile, I heard "IP" and thought it referred to Bruce Lee's teacher, Ip Man. I'd just met Brian a few hours earlier, and he was already firing questions at me like a pyramid-scheme recruiter.

"What's your one-year goal? What's your five-year goal?"

I was like, "Man, I don't even know what I'm doing tomorrow."

Nobody had ever made me think about the future or my career like that. By the end of the photo shoot, Brian had dropped enough gems that he quickly went from a know-it-all stranger to a trustworthy hyung. Eventually, I asked him to be my manager, conveniently timed with the release of my debut album. For once, someone outside my friend group saw what I was doing and thought my potential was worth investing in. That shit meant a lot. It made me start thinking about my next steps in a new light: less freestyle, more preparation.

Although I never studied the business of music, I did have an education in the indie hustle from Project Blowed. I was inspired seeing my OGs selling burned mixtape CDs out of car trunks and pressing their own T-shirts. I simply copied their formula. But what gave me a leg up on the older generation was that I knew how to navigate the Internet. I had built an online presence when MySpace was popping for indie musicians (roughly 2005–9). I not only kept my own page updated with content but also scoured for any possible opportunities. I'd comb through digital flyers for rap events, find out who was performing and promoting, and hit up everyone to try to secure a spot. I'd even perform for free if I had to. As my MySpace friend count multiplied—and finally with an actual recorded album to promote and perform—I began getting inquiries about performances, probably two or three a month. L.A. underground rap shows wanted to book me for chump change; I always took the gig. On the rare occasion that it was an all-Asian bill—like the Asian Hip Hop Summit Tour 2008—I felt like I was light years ahead of the other performers. I created a fake manager email account, fredstern82@aol.com, to field booking requests. I figured having a manager would make me seem more professional when it came time to negotiate fees.

That's around the time the kimchi circuit popped off. I began noticing that a lot of interest came from the Asian American community and student organizations. I had learned the ropes of performing inside grimy bars and hip-hop clubs; never did I expect that my most frequent gigs would soon come from random colleges that would never accept me. But the only real money was in their world, not mine, so I joined it. What initially seemed like a disadvantage—being an Asian kid in hip-hop—actually turned into a niche advantage. This new Asian American generation had grown up following me. They commented on my MySpace page and bought my records. They were in my corner. They wanted to support.

Initially, I was getting a couple grand per show, plus paid travel expenses if we were lucky. It was a lot of dough for me, and this went on for a long time. I was afraid to up my rate, even via a fake manager. Once Brian entered the fold, he was immediately like, "No, we gotta ask for more." I was terrified that the money train would stop. It didn't. With bookings going through Brian, I started to get upward of $5,000 per gig—even accounting for his cut and whatever I gave Zo, it was a huge raise. Whether there were ten people in the crowd or one thousand, I got paid. Whether it was an audience full of Korean Ivy League students or Vietnamese families celebrating Lunar New Year, I got paid. The Dumbfoundead brand started to take off, and I went from scrappy underdog to strategic artist. The music was one thing. But leveling up meant treating this shit like a business.

From Harvard to Harvard

Soon the kimchi circuit became my main source of income. I hopped planes to perform at every university and Asian festival you can think of, from Syracuse to Johns Hopkins, from Indianapolis to Columbus. These events were steadily dropping checks in my pocket, and—even with fucked-up sound systems and subpar mics—I grew better at performing. I'd do comedy bits with the crowd in between songs, cracking jokes at colleges about people's studies and the shitty town they lived in.

"What's your major?" I'd ask some random student in the crowd.

"Communications," he'd respond shyly.

"Well, you better get some bass in your voice if you wanna pass," I'd snap back to roars of laughter.

As part of our performance "package," me and Zo also prided ourselves on freestyling at afterparties. Since I was branded as a weed rapper, every stoner on campus wanted to spark up.

"It's been my dream to smoke with you!" some red-eyed student would exclaim as he approached with a burning joint.

"Dream bigger, man," I'd say, chuckling. But I could never say no because I was grateful for my fan base.

The pinnacle of my kimchi circuit experience came in 2010 at the crown jewel of higher learning. On the brisk spring afternoon before that evening's culture show, the Harvard Korean Association presented me with an official university award for being a trailblazer in the Asian community. It was my first time ever giving a speech. I even wore a dress shirt for the occasion.

"I never expected to be here," I told the assembled students. "You see, I never graduated high school. So, the opportunity to speak at an event honoring college seniors is something that's really foreign to me." The audience laughed. "And ironically, I grew up on Harvard Street in Koreatown, Los Angeles—so from Harvard to Harvard is pretty awesome.

"Performing at Harvard isn't nearly as tough as graduating from Harvard, but it's still a pretty big deal for my Korean mom, who can now casually bring up the fact that her son's gone to Harvard," I said. That line killed.

It was a pretty big deal for me too. I could've given the same speech at any number of the universities where I was invited to perform. I used to have an inferiority complex about studious Asian kids, which turned to resentment—I thought I was better than them, with stupid pride. My sole college experience before the kimchi circuit was when I enrolled in a few classes at Los Angeles City College. But that was the typical community-college experience, sharing classrooms with forty-year-old Armenian women trying to kick-start a second career. When I spent time on actual university campuses, I realized that I would have loved the chance to attend college with people my age and spend those formative years together. Because I dropped out of high school, I never got to experience milestones like prom or graduation. Most of my teenage years were spent hanging out with older guys or kids from broken homes like mine. The kimchi circuit gave me a passport out of Koreatown and into Asian America. And in performing at Asian festivals, I got in touch with the ethnic enclaves in different cities across the country, ones that I never knew existed: the Vietnamese in San Jose, the Chinese in Houston, the Filipinos in Vegas, the Hmong in Minneapolis.

Interacting with non-fuck-up Asians around my age was something new for me. Whether I intended it or not, my persona had evolved into being a major representative for Asian American youth. Many of those kids didn't grow up with a lot of Asian friends, and sometimes they had been the only Asian in their whole school and rediscovered their Asian identity in college. Oddly enough, that too was my experience on the kimchi circuit. I saw what being Asian in America really looked like. These college Asians from two-parent, well-to-do homes with good grades would go absolutely apeshit at my shows and get wrecked at the afterparties.

When these kids approached me after a show, it wasn't just, "I'm a big fan." Many times I'd come face-to-face with the Asian kid who grew up in an all-white neighborhood in, like, Wisconsin, and he'd be like, "Bro, you represent for us. You have no idea what it means to me to see you here." Some of these dudes would damn near cling on to the back of the tour bus so we'd take them along. They grew up nothing like me but still related to what I was doing. At first, it felt like a responsibility I never asked for, because I'd always focused solely on the craft of rapping. I was scared to *mis*represent them. But meeting my fans, I realized they were already drawn to who I was. I didn't have to try to be anyone else.

It's funny. The same community that made me feel like an outsider growing up became my core fanbase.

It's Bigger than Hip-Hop

Growing up in Koreatown, I'd hung around my fair share of Asian gangsters (real ones and wannabes) and their female counterparts—ABGs. This profile I knew very well. But the kimchi circuit introduced me to a whole new set of Asian American archetypes. I've listed them here in ascending order of how strongly they repped Asian culture, in my humble opinion:

- **Parachute kids.** They were a subset of FOBs who were dropped into the US by their parents (hence, "parachute") to get an American education on their own. They tended to be driven, independent, and tough, while also exhibiting a curiosity about all things American culture—like rap music.
- **Whitewashed Asians.** These were the kids who grew up in mostly white towns (often in the Midwest), where a new jar of kimchi was over an hour's drive away. They

typically felt alienated from their Asian identities until arriving on a campus with a strong Asian community that embraced them. Born-again Asians, I call them.

- **Wasians + Blasians.** In the Koreatown of my generation, Koreans of mixed race were a rare Pokémon. Running through the kimchi circuit around the country, I came across more mixed Asians than I'd ever seen. Some were from military families, and Wasians (white + Asian) were the most popular variation—and almost all had white dads and Asian moms, rarely the other way around. Like whitewashed Asians, many of them had to minimize their Asianness to fit in in their hometowns but were free to wave their flags—or half of them, anyway—proudly on campus.
- **Adoptees.** I would always be shocked to meet a Korean guy who looked like a James Kim and find out his name was Tyler Johnson. Asians adopted into white families went *extra* hard on their Asian identity, and I can't blame them—many were often unable to connect deeply with their ethnic roots, even with well-meaning parents. As these adoptees got older, they were extra diligent about discovering the culture that those of us who grew up in Asian households took for granted. You keep on repping, Tyler.
- **Asian American Christians.** This group included people from all the above categories—mostly KAs, since Korean churches in America became de facto networking hubs for immigrants. Among their kids, the spectrum ran

from devout Bible thumpers to those who party all night Saturday and stumble bleary-eyed into Sunday service.

This list is meant to be somewhat humorous, but at the same time, it surprised me how much I appealed to all these different groups of Asians. Before the kimchi circuit, I thought my rap style wasn't something Asian kids could be proud of. I wasn't aggressive or hard like 2Pac, not a ladies' man like LL, never a smooth hustler like Jay-Z. I wasn't even one of those artsy-fartsy, spoken-word "yellow rage" rappers you might see dripping with righteous anger on *Def Poetry Jam*. I didn't look like the face of representation. If anything, I looked like the poster child for a "Stay in School" campaign. But I soon learned that my success in battle rap galvanized the Asian American community—my wins became our collective wins. As my battle clips circulated, Asian kids saw how I took down people of all races—not with violence or tough talk, but with punchlines, humor, and wit. They respected that. And when I defended myself against the tired insults they'd probably heard their entire lives, it was as if I were defending not just myself, but all of them. It gave me a lane, and my confidence in the arena gave them confidence in being marginalized. And even more than my predecessor Jin, I needed the Asian community's support. I didn't have a major label or an established rap crew standing behind me.

The more I traversed Asian America, the more I realized that it was bigger than hip-hop (word to dead prez). When I started representing something bigger than the craft itself—the power of Asian identity and community—my persona became more than the neighborhood stoner who could rhyme his ass off. It was a new version of myself whom I actually *liked*. I had already won the approval of fellow rapper peers, but this newfound popularity was something different. Dumbfoundead was a cooler, less-bullied version of me. Not the kid from the fucked-up household or the high-school dropout trying to escape Koreatown. But someone with juice, fans, and influence.

When you're Asian in hip-hop, you grow up hearing you're a guest in the culture. And I did feel that way at first. But after a while, I stopped feeling like one. I felt like I belonged. I was one of the few Asian rappers *in* the culture, not just posting typed bars on message boards. The attention and acclaim I got on the kimchi circuit boosted my self-esteem. I wasn't an outsider in hip-hop anymore, and I wasn't crashing the Asian community's party either. I was just myself, and both sides accepted me. It felt good. But after a while, the approval didn't hit the same.

Graduation

Around then came Nora Lum, aka Awkwafina. The music video for her song "My Vag"—a profane, funny anthem about her vagina—dropped on YouTube in October 2012. I was drawn to her as soon as I saw it, the way I'm always curious about any Asian American who is making interesting art. When I see exciting Asian talent, I immediately think, *How can we work together? How can I help make them bigger?* I want to surround myself with fresh energy and contribute to it in some way.

I'd never seen an Asian woman like Awkwafina. She was quirky, honest, and self-deprecating—the vibe of an awkward New York hipster, but in a charming way. Beyond her unique look and sound, what impressed me most was her creative vision. At first, I wasn't sure if she was a comedian doing troll rap songs or if she wanted to be an actual musician. Right after the "My Vag" video came out, I hit her up on Facebook Messenger, and we started talking. She already knew about me, and her video director, Court Dunn, was a fan of mine too. We stayed in touch, and she came to one of my New York shows—a tiny woman rocking oversized glasses, a beanie, and a vintage Mets shirt. I quickly realized she was legit—incredibly smart and naturally funny. Nora was a straight-up stoner, but also had a neurotic, high-energy Queens vibe: quick-witted, sharp-tongued, and unfiltered, like one of the homies. She wasn't trying to be the coolest or the hardest; therefore, she seemed like an outcast while everyone around her was overcompensating. It was like meeting the female version of me—if the female version of me had the raspy voice of someone who'd smoked a hundred cartons of cigarettes before her eighteenth birthday. (Little did I know she'd go on to become one of the most sought-after voice actors of our time. Seriously, she's voiced more animated birds than Gilbert Gottfried.) Nora and I instantly hit it off and became friends. Some months later, she posted about the availability of a subletted room in her Greenpoint apartment in Brooklyn. So, I moved in with Nora for a few months in 2013, the longest stretch I ever lived in New York. (This period was immortalized in my song "Brooklyn for a Month.") Nora's apartment was railroad-style, which meant the rooms were all connected to each other—you had to walk through one to get to another. Her boyfriend at the time, this impossibly tall white dude named Peter, would have to go through my room to get to the kitchen for a glass of orange juice.

Living as roommates, Nora and I got close, like a pair of stoner siblings. She wasn't a freestyle rapper, but a very calculated artist, writing and producing all her songs and recording them herself. She knew her way around all the tech gear and was super hands-on with her recording process—much more than I was. Nora had a specific picture in her mind of how she wanted her music and videos to look and sound. And she was doing it all on her own, independently, and not making much money. I was struck by the clarity of her artistic goals. She had momentum from "My Vag" and another song called "Yellow Ranger," and was performing shows around the underground Brooklyn music scene. Since I had been in the game for a while by then, I was able to pass on some of my knowledge about turning music into a business: shipping CDs, printing and selling merch, and making a living off it. But what I really put her on to was connecting with her Asian heritage—and the kimchi circuit.

Nora's Korean mother passed away from an illness when she was only four. She was raised by her Chinese dad and grandma. Still, even as a New York native from Queens, she was more in tune with the hipster artist scene than Asian culture or the Asian American community. I saw an opportunity: Because I was getting paid so well on the kimchi circuit, I figured it would be easy money for her. I took her to Ktown, in both NYC and L.A., and introduced her to the people and the spaces that would soon embrace her. Before long, she was getting kimchi-circuit dates of her own. As they did for me, her shows tapped into a whole new audience and connected her more deeply to her Asian upbringing. I could sense in her a new level of confidence. If anything, those Asian American kids gravitated even more toward Nora than they did to me. They saw what I saw when I first watched "My Vag"—someone original and inscrutable, with a tomboyish presentation that both guys and girls were drawn to. In 2015, Nora and I joined forces for a college tour with DJ Zo called "Fresh Off the Books"—a maybe-not-so-clever ode to Eddie Huang's book and TV show *Fresh Off the Boat*. The tour was essentially a formalized version of the kimchi circuit, hitting a dozen or so universities over a couple months. It was chaotic and fun and on our own terms.

For Nora, it was clearly just a pit stop on her way to greater things. While I'd been more or less content running the college circuit, she was getting book deals, Comedy Central gigs, and hosting her own YouTube talk show. I saw her star rise in real time. Nora phased out of the kimchi circuit within two years, while I was stuck in it for eight years running. She figured out her path and went from being an offbeat broke Asian girl in Brooklyn to making serious moves in the industry. Seeing how quickly she transitioned out of the circuit made me realize I'd been stuck in it for too long. I began to feel boxed in by the same thing that had once set me free. I was a repeat performer at the same colleges and festivals where I'd once enjoyed the novelty of new fans. Like Matthew McConaughey's line from *Dazed and Confused*, I was getting older, and they were staying the same age. (Except it didn't make me laugh.) My friends in the L.A. scene, like Anderson .Paak and TOKiMONSTA, were getting mainstream notoriety and playing big festivals. Meanwhile, I was getting calls from Boston College, not Bonnaroo. The checks were still decent, but the ceiling was closing in. Was I turning into an updated version of the taekwondo team, with a third-degree black belt in college shows? I talked to Brian, and we decided that I'd set a new, higher rate. If the schools wouldn't match it, I wouldn't do the gig. After that, the number of dates dwindled, but at least I was betting on my worth. There were younger Asian American MCs who could take those gigs. It was time to push myself in new directions.

The Chitlin' Circuit faded once African American musicians realized there was more money to be made performing for white audiences. Segregation had become less of a barrier, and more of America got exposed to Black music. For me, the kimchi circuit gave my budding career a huge boost, not only in funds but also in how I saw myself as an artist and as an Asian American. I didn't need to reject the kimchi circuit, but I did need to outgrow it. I needed something bigger than being big in Asian America. If I wanted to keep evolving, I had to go where it all started.

CHAPTER TEN

BACK TO THE MOTHERLAND

Growing up, I knew Korean American kids who took annual summer pilgrimages to Korea to visit their extended families. I loved my carefree L.A. summers way too much to envy them. I pictured sweaty children running alongside the Han River on a humid day, catching dragonflies in a net. Maybe afterward, they'd sit outside a corner shop and eat a patbingsoo to cool down in the sticky heat. At night, they'd lie on a wooden floor in their halmoni's house in a room with no A/C, swatting mosquitoes while a noisy fan whirred in a corner. When these kids returned to L.A., they never had exciting tales of life-changing experiences to share about their trips. After all, when you're a kid and you go to Korea with your parents, you're stuck with them and all the aunts and uncles you're required to visit. Overseas relatives might be your blood, but they're basically strangers.

I couldn't relate, because I never took one of those summer Korea trips. Both of my parents were mostly estranged from their respective families in Korea, and it's not like my father was going to spend the money to take us there—or anywhere—for a family vacation. So, I didn't visit Korea until I was twenty-three. Although I was curious, I never had a burning desire to go to the motherland, which I associated with visiting grandparents who smelled of ginseng and mothballs. Besides, I had a little bit of fear about the unfamiliar world outside of L.A. Trapped in my rap bubble, I was hyperfocused on realizing my American dream, not reconnecting with my Korean roots. What was happening in Korea wasn't even a blip on my radar.

But since my first trip to Korea in 2009, I've gone back every year. In the beginning, it was always some sort of paid gig that brought me there—a hosting job, a festival, or a collab with a Korean artist. I even filmed a series of YouTube videos at historic sites for the Korea Tourism Organization. Until recently, nearly all my global travel was work-related. When the bookings in Korea slowed, I started flying myself out.

And it wasn't to catch dragonflies at the Han River. Nor was it to brush up on my language skills at Yonsei University's famed summer program for Korean American students. By going to Korea in my early twenties, I skipped out on family and schooling and jumped headfirst into Seoul's budding hip-hop scene and hipster subculture. That initial trip coincided with another movement starting to take hold in the capital city. A community of Korean American adults around my age were at the forefront of a mini reverse migration: returning to the homeland of their parents to pursue their dreams. These weren't people who were content to teach English for a couple of years or land corporate-stiff jobs at Samsung or LG. No, these were Korean Americans just like me—children of immigrants who wanted to make a living in a creative industry. Except they went to do it in Seoul, not in America. These reverse migrants—my peers, the cool kids—would form a network of friends that helped me further establish my base in Seoul.

I kept going back to Korea for a variety of reasons, but overall, I just found it a comforting place. Being in Korea felt like taking off sneakers and slipping into some slides. There's some male privilege in that, which we'll get into, but I attribute it mostly to my identity as a Korean American. There are countless KA books, essays, and podcast episodes that touch on a tiresome cliché: "I'm not Korean enough for Korea and not American enough for America, so I don't fit in anywhere." That perceived lack of acceptance is always framed as a disadvantage for a gyopo, the Korean term for a person of Korean descent who grew up overseas. But fuck the cliché. If you tilt the frame, you might see that being Korean American can actually be a superpower: The ability to credibly tap into both cultures gives you an advantage. Rather than focusing on how you're not accepted, you can carve out a unique lane. Some of my close friends—like Jay Park, for one—have taken that route in Korea and achieved great success. The overwhelming global popularity of Netflix's *KPop Demon Hunters*, powered almost entirely by gyopos, is another case in point. In Korea, I learned how to connect both sides of my Korean American identity. I also found love, inspiration—and a little bit of trouble.

B-Boys, Drugs & Hyungs

Breakdancing first brought me to Korea in 2009—ironic, considering I can't breakdance for shit. I knew a Ktown noona named Alice Han whose friends had moved to Seoul and launched a B-boy competition called R-16. As with other disciplines, once Korea became a global competitor in breakdancing, the government started pumping money into it. Within a couple of years, thanks to government funding, R-16 became one of the biggest annual breakdancing festivals in the world, inviting B-boy crews from sixteen countries to participate. The third R-16 was to take place in late September 2009 in Incheon, about twenty miles southwest of Seoul. Alice introduced me to R-16's co-organizers—two gyopos from New York named Charlie and Johnjay—and they asked me if I wanted to perform at the event. A free trip to Korea just to rap? They didn't have to ask twice.

The lineup of performers featured the "godfather" of Korean hip-hop, Tiger JK, and his group Drunken Tiger, as well as Korean rap vets Epik High. The imports on the bill included Rakaa Iriscience of the L.A. underground group Dilated Peoples, who is one quarter Korean; Roscoe Umali, a Filipino American rapper and ex-Drunken Tiger member (who later got caught up in a mortgage scam and is now doing fed time); and me, the youngest performer, and one of the only Korean American MCs making noise in the States. I was thrilled for the opportunity. It was my first-ever trip outside of the country—and it was on someone else's dime. I was curious to check out the Korean hip-hop scene. I knew a few of the big Korean rap groups by name—Drunken Tiger, Epik High, and Dynamic Duo—but I hadn't listened to their music. Otherwise, I had no knowledge of the scene whatsoever. If I'm being honest, I wasn't expecting much. What could they possibly be rapping about? The stress from college entrance exams and chasing down opps on the mean streets of Hongdae?

About a week before I left for Korea, another Korean American rapper from L.A.—let's call him Steve—hit me up.

"Yo, I heard you're going to Korea," Steve said, "and I want to go too."

I told him, "I can't cover your flight or anything, but if you pull up, we can all hang out together."

I wasn't especially close with Steve, but I wanted someone I knew to roll with overseas, so I encouraged him to join. So, Steve pulled the trigger and bought a plane ticket to Korea.

After I arrived in Incheon and settled into my hotel, I texted Steve to meet up. He was staying at the same spot. When I saw him in the lobby, I could tell he was super hyped to share something with me. I asked him what was up, and he leaned in.

"Bro," he said in a conspiratorial whisper, "I snuck in thirty ecstasy pills with me."

I blinked. "The fuck? How did you do that?"

I was abusing all kinds of substances in L.A., but I came to Korea empty-handed because I had heard how strict they were about drugs. Steve, however, was undeterred; he double-wrapped thirty E pills into a condom and tucked them into . . . well, let's just say he wasn't sitting too comfortably in 29E. Visibly stoked at sneaking his stash through airport security, Steve described how he planned to sell the pills for a profit through some local connections. I didn't ponder the risk too deeply; my only thought was, *Oh shit, we're gonna roll on E at Korean clubs!* At that moment, my mind was elsewhere, excited for the week ahead.

Besides, whatever Steve was up to was secondary to my main responsibility in Korea: R-16 weekend. In Incheon, I saw up close the power of Korean B-boys. There was a pint-sized twelve-year-old named Pocket who could do the most aerial spins in the world—he had an insane, almost superhuman ability to defy gravity. Breakdancing might have been fading in popularity in the States, but in Korea, it was thriving. They took the art form and ran with it, pushing the limits in ways I hadn't seen before. Korea has always jumped in on trends they didn't originate—everything from fashion to music to fried chicken—but once they commit to something, they go all in. And when Koreans realized they could dominate B-boying, it became serious. It's a discipline that rewards practice, and Koreans practice *hard*—it's embedded in the culture. Whether it's breakdancing or academics, there's always that mindset of *How can we become the best at this? How can we prove ourselves on a global stage?* That's how Korean B-boys became top-tier—treating it not as a hobby, but a discipline.

At R-16, it was my first time hearing people say my rap name in Korean—덤파운데드, which phonetically sounds more like "Dum-pah-oon-ded-uh"—or "Dum-pah" for short. I was getting recognized not only by Koreans but also by B-boys and graffiti artists who had traveled from as far as Russia, Brazil, and the Netherlands. People seemed surprised that I was even in Korea. The kimchi circuit had proven that I had pull with Asian Americans, but coming to Korea unlocked a new international fan base. It was then that I truly grasped the global reach of YouTube. My Internet rap battles made me recognizable—people from all over knew my face from freestyling and battling. Seeing the traction I had was wild, and a real boost to my ego.

To my surprise, even Tiger JK—twelve years my senior and a stone-cold legend of Korean rap—had heard of me. I knew his name because there were Ktown kids who listened to his music, which stood out compared to other Korean rap because it was more explicit and edgy. Beyond the music, the myth surrounding JK was that he was a fearless rebel who used his black belt in taekwondo to rough up people in street fights. When I first met him at R-16, I bowed with respect. "Yo, it's an honor to meet, I heard a lot about you." I was kind of expecting him to have a FOB swag, but his English was perfect. I was shocked to discover that he had lived in L.A. during his teenage years in the early nineties and attended Beverly Hills High School with famed hip-hop producer The Alchemist. JK had even gone to Project Blowed, the same open mic I used to go to, but years before my time. His L.A. upbringing, amid the '92 riots and heyday of West Coast gangsta rap, is why Drunken Tiger's albums resonated in American ears. We clicked fast. JK told me that I reminded him of himself, which I considered a high compliment. We've kept in touch since that first meeting, and I still text him sometimes for advice to this day.

JK was a true big brother figure—a real hyung. Being in Korea was my first time getting truly hyunged. Hyung means "older brother" in Korean, but it is used by men to address any older man they associate with, whether biologically related or not. By Korean tradition, I would call any guy friend who's older than me—even if only by a year—my hyung and address him that way. In American slang, it's something like "OG." Hyungs use the term dongsaeng to refer to younger people. I never liked using those terms in America because there were plenty of Korean guys older than me who I thought were total losers, not worthy of any special respect. But hyung hits different in Korea, where Confucian respect for elders is basically codified.

It was cool to meet a Korean rap hyung in person, but I was still short on making actual friends in Korea. I did, however, have some new R-16 buddies, all of whom were visiting Korea for the first time like me. Like my roommate Brent Rollins, a prolific NYC-based, L.A.-raised graphic designer who created the logos for the films *Boyz n the Hood, Poetic Justice,* and *Mo' Better Blues,* as well as for rap groups like Dilated Peoples. Along with Brent, I mobbed around with Pose and Ewok, two members of the L.A.-based MSK graffiti crew. I also befriended a couple of guys from Korea's top breakdancing team, Rivers Crew. After long days watching B-boys spin into the night, we'd all hop on the train to Seoul and dive into the chaos.

Itaewon and Hongdae were the two main neighborhoods in Seoul where we went to party. Itaewon, close to the Yongsan military base where US soldiers had been stationed since the Korean War, was a hotbed for foreigners and the nexus of youth culture. It's where we'd see African vendors crossing paths with halal food–selling Turks, all while young people of every ethnicity partied until the sun rose. Hongdae, which had fewer foreigners, was where university kids and young club-hoppers would roam around in thirsty packs every night. Running around Itaewon, I met non-American gyopos for the first time—Korean British, Korean Canadians, and others from across the diaspora. They recognized me too. It boggled my mind that I would have Korean fans from all over the world. I'll never forget the first time I heard a Korean Australian speak. I was with Brent and crew chatting up girls in some seedy Itaewon alley, when suddenly this pretty Korean face opened her mouth and out came the thickest Aussie accent I'd ever heard: "Annyeonghaseyaur." It was like seeing Steve Irwin reincarnated as a K-pop idol—it completely blew my

Ktown mind. The diversity in Seoul—Itaewon especially—opened me up to Korea in a new way. I underestimated the range of its culture, thinking everything was going to resemble the cheesy nightspots and karaoke bars I avoided in Ktown. In L.A., clubs close at two, but Korea is infamous for its all-nighters. I collected wristbands like souvenirs from clubs like nb in Hongdae and Club Heaven in Gangnam. Leaving at sunrise, still buzzed, I'd step over suited-up businessmen—all somehow drunker than me—lying prone on the sidewalk. I'd just had the night of my life; for them, it was just another Wednesday.

There were plenty of cavernous EDM-bumping megaclubs around Seoul, but subcultures, especially those related to hip-hop, were starting to take off around that time. The DJ collective 360 Sounds was pivotal to that growth. They specialized in playing deep rap cuts and old-school samples and throwing all the best parties. Once the R-16 team introduced me to them, I immediately got tapped into the under-the-radar bars and clubs of Seoul nightlife. They put me on to rare vinyl that the American homies weren't even up on. (Once again, they studied the shit out of us.) 360 members like DJ Soulscape and Plastic Kid were not only my hyungs but also the OGs of the cool Seoul party scene.

They also introduced me to the slightly scary side of the hyung relationship, because part of being a hyung is keeping your dongsaengs in check. Whenever I started acting a little ridiculous or arrogant, my big bro who'd been acting all nice to me would instantly switch into angry hyung mode, like, "You fucking little disrespectful fuck." (Drinking always amplified this playful aggression.) Hyungs will act like the hierarchy isn't that important to them, until suddenly it is.

When I first got to know Plastic Kid, he told me, "Yeah, you don't have to call me hyung." But then I might roast him the way I would any homie, and he'd quickly remind me, "I'm your hyung." Basically: Don't get it twisted, you better listen to what I say. I grew to understand how essential the hyung/dongsaeng dynamic is to the culture.

I got hyunged pretty hard that trip. Remember my friend Steve and the thirty ecstasy pills? I guess he talked to one too many people, because someone got nicked by the police and snitched on him. (Ratting out a drug dealer is basically a national sport in Korea.) Next thing you know, Steve's room at the hotel got raided, and he was arrested. At first, when one of the R-16 hyungs told me what went down, I brushed it off like it was a small thing. My hyungs didn't mince words: If Steve told the police he was here for R-16, it could tarnish the festival's name, and they could lose their government funding. It was a dumb move by Steve, and it could've fucked up the whole festival. I didn't tell him to bring drugs, but I still felt responsible because he came to Korea on my account. Steve ended up getting locked up in Korea for three months, then paid a bunch of lawyer fees to get out of the country. He got banned from reentering Korea for ten years, but it could've been much worse. R-16 survived.

When Steve was first arrested, my hyungs told me I should probably leave Korea. I didn't. I just checked into a different hotel and remained paranoid for the rest of the trip. Thankfully, I stayed, because if I hadn't, I never would've met my first true love.

Kyuhee

At the first 360 Sounds party I ever attended, I fell instantly in love—not just with the club, but with Seoul itself. For the first time since arriving, I felt truly at home. The place had an alternative energy that was familiar to a lifelong Angeleno. The people milling around the bar looked straight out of a streetwear ad, mingling to jazzy hip-hop, tattooed and pierced, dressed in vintage fits. As I scanned the crowd, my eyes were immediately drawn to a cute, petite girl in a vintage blue dress. Underneath short bangs, she wore a septum ring, tattoo sleeves running down both arms. To be fair, Seoul's streets were teeming with impossibly pretty women who turned my head all week. But because of the ubiquity of plastic surgery, there's an archetypal look sometimes called the "Gangnam face"—and unfortunately, I'm less attracted to that face. (If they chose, say, a "Bushwick face," I'd be in heaven.) Suffice it to say, the girl at the 360 party did not.

I ordered a beer, took a nervous swig, and sauntered toward her to strike up a conversation. It's not my usual MO to holler at a random girl at a club—I usually need a wingman or a lot of liquid courage—so I was nervous. Back at home, I probably wouldn't even have approached her. However, I felt cockier in Korea. In L.A., I'd always assumed Korean Americans like me were cooler and more daring than FOBs—so in Seoul, I felt a little like Superman surrounded by Clark Kents. Call it a misguided American superiority complex, but it gave me the audacity to step to Miss Vintage Blue Dress and introduce myself.

I started to stammer in Korean, because I thought she might be a native. "Annyeonghaseyo, Jon imnida."

She responded with a smirk, "Relax, I speak English."

I took a deep breath and smiled.

She told me her name was Kyuhee, and I soon found out that she was a gyopo from Cali, a pastor's kid who once lived on a commune, graduated from UC Davis, and had just moved to Seoul to study for her master's degree. She'd just turned twenty-three, same as me. The way she looked, spoke, and carried herself, she was the coolest chick in the room: artsy, sexy, and mysterious. I told her I was a rapper from L.A. in town to perform at R-16. She had no idea who I was, which was refreshing because it meant I was winning her over on charm alone. We kept talking and drinking and instantly hit it off. A couple of hours later, we were making out drunk on the streets of Itaewon. I was supposed to go back to L.A. in twenty-four hours, but boarding a plane felt impossible to even consider.

For the first time—and it definitely wouldn't be the last—I impulsively extended my stay on the eve of a Korea departure. (Why is it so hard to leave this place?) Kyuhee was the first girl I had a real, obsessive crush on. Sure, I'd experienced more one-night stands since my rap career took off, but Kyu gave me an entirely different feeling. Something like . . . love. Drunk hookups were familiar, but during the days that followed, the only buzz came from simply being together. We went out to eat, visited museums, and frolicked around Seoul like a KA version of *Before Sunrise*—inseparable.

Kyuhee challenged me. I paraded through life thinking I had the coolest, edgiest taste in culture, but Kyu was one battle I couldn't win. Every time I tried to wow her with a reference, she knew about it already. If I played her the most obscure song I liked, she would say, "Oh, I have the original vinyl for that." She was extremely smart and stylish and could drink and party with literally anyone—a girl who was feminine and soft but loved hanging with the boys. With that came a confidence I found intoxicatingly attractive.

That week, I also had the opportunity to rap in front of her—not at a concert, but for an in-studio YouTube show called *Mic Swagger,* hosted by Sool J, one of the top freestylers in Korea. I wore a 360 Sounds T-shirt that I got earlier that week, and when I grabbed the mic, I went off like I was back at Project Blowed: *Mic Swagger, I am a nice rapper, I might slap ya, maybe we can fight after.* I probably went extra hard because I knew Kyuhee was watching, like hoopers who turn it up a notch when their girl is in the stands.

We had still only made out with each other up until my final night in Seoul. Kyuhee was staying with her grandmother, so we decided to sneak into her halmoni's apartment after a night of drinking, Kyuhee leading the way like we were two spies behind enemy lines. After we made love for a very passionate six minutes, we lay together in the dim morning light, lost in our own thoughts. Without even saying it, we knew that the intimacy of the moment—and of the previous week—had been meaningful. But it was time to say goodbye. I snuck back out into the Seoul morning, wandering the empty streets alone in the brisk autumn air, reflecting on my first trip to the motherland. I was super sad to leave, and it wasn't only because of Kyuhee. Korea was somehow everything I expected—the food, the convenience, the comfort of everyone looking like me—and an entirely different world that I never imagined, where youth culture felt alive and new. Like many Korean Americans who visit and have similar experiences, I began fantasizing about what life would be like if I moved to Seoul for real. It was a feeling I had every time I came to Korea for the first few years—a feeling I was forced to snap out of when I returned to the States.

Kyuhee was a glimpse of a Korean American who had relocated to Korea and created a life for herself as a gyopo. I consider her one of the first members of this reverse migration of cool Korean Americans back to Seoul. She wasn't alone. Other like-minded gyopos had relocated too—Ben and Luke, who started the video agency The Cut; Terrence and Kevin Kim, two brothers behind the clothing line IISE; and Sohyun Lim, an illustrator/graphic designer. This new generation wasn't just fucking around in Seoul to party their summer breaks away; they were putting down roots to pursue creative endeavors. It gave me a ready-made crew of KA locals—including fashion people, videographers, and DJs—whenever I visited Korea.

When I got back to L.A., Kyuhee and I agreed to not communicate with each other digitally—no texts, emails, or social media—and only corresponded via handwritten letter. (I know. So cheesy.) So, for a couple of years, we snail-mailed letters to each other every month, like a modern-day Frida and Diego. Kyuhee was so poetic. She'd make mundane observations of passersby on the streets come alive through her words, like I was right beside her: "I got 2 men standing in front of me, both dressed in black suits, shiny black shoes, the man on the left has a magenta bejeweled necktie & the man on the right has a sea scene blue-green dazzling tie. HAHA. Both have bellies like they swallow the SOJU every fucking night . . . ROOM SALON style." She'd also send perfumed handkerchiefs and playfully risqué photos of her posing in some state of undress by a mirror. "You're pretty fucking sweet for an 'emotionally challenged' guy," she wrote. "You're an atypical Ktown boy." Meanwhile, I sent her postcards scribbled with random tales of tour hijinks from weird towns like Weed, California. More than once, I expressed my desire to fully relocate to Korea. "This tour definitely confirmed my desire to move there," I wrote in November 2009. "I'm in need of new inspirations and challenges."

Inevitably, the heat of our romance cooled with the long distance—but through our letters we became closer friends too; we traded dating misadventures and gave each other brutally honest relationship advice. (I've jokingly called Kyu the "Erykah Badu of gyopos"—meaning there's always a flock of cool creative guys trailing closely behind her, trying to win her affection.) A few years ago, I scanned all of our old letters and published them as a zine. You can never forget the first person who made you feel that way, right? Knowing Kyuhee made Korea feel a little less foreign. When I returned for R-16 the next summer, it felt like I was stepping onto familiar ground.

The Hongdae Cypher

In the summer of 2010, I went back to Seoul with a battery in my back, fresh off the drop of a new collaborative album (*Wax & DFD Are Clockwise*). For that year's R-16, to be held in Seoul, I was tapped to host, and I brought DJ Zo with me. We arrived in Korea in late June, and I started delving deeper into the hip-hop scene, feeling a new kind of love. Upon returning to the States the previous summer, I'd uploaded vlogs of my '09 Korea trip on YouTube, and apparently the Koreans were watching. Being called a legend by Koreans was flattering in a way I hadn't anticipated. Hearing that kind of compliment from your own people is damn near like getting praised by family. I had become accustomed to fans in the States running up on me and shouting, "Oh shit, you're Dumbfoundead. Can I get a picture?" In Korea, those moments of recognition were quieter, slower, yet somehow twice as impactful. That motherland love hits different. When passing by groups of Korean teenagers, I'd hear muted whispers of "Ohhhhh??" slowly build to a crescendo—almost like an expression of shock. When people seemed shy or intimidated to approach me, I felt like an actual celebrity.

It was a World Cup summer, which meant the Seoul streets were alive with fans of the national team decked out in red. In Hongdae, there was a playground in a bustling area that was known for its buskers. On my first trip, I'd made a mental note passing by, thinking, *That would be a perfect spot for a cypher.* So, in 2010 I decided to host a get-together there. This was the era of the surprise social-media pop-up, when taco trucks would announce where they'd be stationed for the day on the morning of. I used that strategy to post a Facebook blast announcing a spontaneous meetup for rappers. The flyer featured a black-and-white portrait of my face with a sign over my mouth that read, "CALLING ALL MCs" in English over Korean words that translated to "Let's chill at Hongdae Playground. Let's pass the mic around." I billed it as the "1st Annual Dumbfoundead + 친구들의 Freestyle Session—Dumbfoundead + Friends—at Hongdae Playground" on June 27, 2010, from "7 p.m. till the Cops Shut Us Down."

At the hotel, Zo loaded up dozens of freestyle instrumentals onto his laptop. I wasn't sure what to expect at Hongdae Playground, but when we pulled up, I was taken aback to see hundreds of kids awaiting our arrival. Zo connected his laptop to a portable-speaker setup, and the cypher ignited. I had culture shock seeing Korean kids jump in the circle and rap so confidently—and well. Footage exists from that June afternoon in Hongdae, and eagle-eyed K-rap fans can probably spot a few notable faces jumping in the cypher: Justhis, DPR Live, and

Huckleberry P—all of whom went on to have successful rap careers.

I was the conductor of the symphony, encouraging people to join the cypher and spit—but of course, as the ringleader, I had to participate too. The young Korean rappers were good, but I had much more experience, plus the cockiness I earned from running the gauntlet at Project Blowed. Once I had conquered that intimidating environment, I could jump into any cypher. At Blowed, you had to cut someone off to get a word in; here, cultural deference still reigned supreme. It's a funny quirk of Korean rap—a genre known for aggression and rebellion against authority—because social etiquette demands politeness, forcing even spitters to stay cordial to strangers. This meant each MC graciously yielded the floor to the next, and everyone kowtowed to me. I even threw in some bars in Korean, despite not being fluent. Lacking native fluency in Korean has never prevented me from using it whenever I need to. The only way to learn how to communicate effectively in a different language is to accept sounding imperfect and be confident in your delivery—a lot like freestyling. So, I was rapping in broken Korean without giving a fuck. That's hip-hop. I soaked in the rewarding sounds of *oohs* and *aahs* from the crowd, except the Korean version, so a little higher pitched. After the cypher ended, scores of girls crowded around me for selfies and autographs. It felt surreal, like I'd just bridged some cultural gap in the cypher. If they didn't know me before, they definitely knew who Dumbfoundead was now.

Throughout that trip, Seoul nightlife sucked me in even further. I loved it all—the women, the drinking, the . . . um, after-hours adventures. I was still cool with Kyuhee but free to do my own thing. Hookup culture felt simpler, less performative in Korea. Fewer expectations, clearer rules. After clubbing all night, there were always people ready to pair up once the lights turned on. Unlike in America, most Koreans in their twenties still live with their parents. And there I was, a hotshot foreigner coming in with my own hotel room—well, actually, the first couple of years I was sharing rooms, so I would take girls to love motels that charged hourly rates. I enjoyed mingling with a whole new type of woman, because I was so used to dating loud L.A. ABGs. Hearing "oppa" whispered in my ear in bed for the first time really got me going. I wasn't sure how to respond; they don't teach you how to dirty talk in Korean school.

I started to wonder why my Korean parents decided to immigrate to America—and to settle in Koreatown of all places. It's like they chose Korea*town* over Korea*world*—a knockoff Korea with a fentanyl problem. Surprisingly, spending time in Korea gave me a better understanding of my father—and not in a good way. I had seen the effect of his behavior through my mom, but in Korea I saw the root cause. The patriarchal society gives a lot of leeway to men. Middle-aged men, in particular, act like they're above the law—hell, half the time they think they *are* the law. It was no wonder Korean American men loved going to Korea so much. Gender roles felt more traditional. It was like living in Don Draper's America. I was wilin' out but feeling guilty. I was reaping the benefits of the imbalanced power dynamic—privileges I'd never earned—and catching uncomfortable glimpses of my father's entitlement mirrored in my own behavior. Even when I was speaking Korean I started sounding like my dad.

I also began to understand why gyopos can get a bad rep among native Koreans in Seoul. I was sensitive to the stereotype of over-the-top Korean Americans wearing out their welcome. But it's ironic that I had to go to Korea to realize how annoying Ktown people can be—and not just your regular, everyday Ktown person, but the *worst* kind of irritating archetype—the "More shots!" and "What the hell you looking at, fool?" type. Like how the British sent their convicts to Australia—except our exports to Korea came with spiky haircuts, bad tattoos, and shitty attitudes. Over the years, I noticed some of the Ktown homies moving out to Korea. Some were involved in criminal activity in the States and had to flee the country; others just had nothing going for them in L.A., so they wanted to move somewhere they could afford an aimless lifestyle.

Not all gyopos were like this, mind you. I heard an acronym used by some Korean Americans to refer to others in their subset: NBH. It's a pejorative to describe those Korean Americans who go to Korea acting like they're the shit just because they're from the US—most commonly, from L.A. or New York. (Or more accurately, from Orange County or Long Island.) But in reality, they are NBH: Nobody Back Home. They come to Korea and forge a whole new identity for themselves, boasting about degrees and celebrity friendships nobody could verify. NBHs lie with impunity. Sure, you can find some real Korean American gangstas in pockets of Seoul, but I've seen gyopos in Gangnam cosplaying the Dogg Pound in Dickie shorts and Nike Cortez, throwing up gang signs and dropping the N-bomb without any consequences. (And I don't mean 니가.)

I've already mentioned the "cool kid" gyopos like Kyuhee who had relocated to Seoul to do creative work. But among all the Korean Americans rising in Seoul, one group stood out the most to me, probably because I saw myself in them most directly: the rapper gyopos.

Show Me the Money

In 2012, a hip-hop reality competition premiered on the Korean network Mnet. At the time, it was the only hip-hop show on Korean TV. That program, with the somewhat cringey, *Jerry Maguire*–biting title *Show Me the Money,* would become a juggernaut over its eleven seasons. It was basically *American Idol* and *The Voice* mashed up with *Squid Game,* with tens of thousands of aspiring MCs from public auditions narrowed down into small teams, each assigned to a celebrity rapper/producer duo. By season's end, after countless performance competitions and battles, there is one final winner. Many credit the popularity of *Show Me the Money* for rap's explosive growth in Korea in the 2010s; it made stars out of winners like Loco, BewhY, and Nafla. But *Show Me* was so big that even those who didn't win the top prize—names like BIG Naughty, Sik-K, Woo Won-jae, and Nucksal—became nationally famous.

Because hip-hop is an American invention, it was only natural that *Show Me the Money* would invite Korean American competitors, even if they didn't grow up in Korea and had a weak grasp of the native tongue. It's similar to how athletes can compete for a different country in the Olympics or the FIFA World Cup through ancestry. Year after year, as *Show Me the Money* became increasingly popular, I watched many of my Korean American peers try out for the show. Most never advanced past the audition stage, but a few of them made it pretty far. Though no Korean American has ever won the final prize (or been a runner-up), *Show Me the Money* helped launch viable Korean rap careers for some of them—friends of mine like G2 from Dallas, Flowsik from NY, and Junoflo from L.A. Even if they were never going to win, by virtue of being American and a rapper, they had a trump card: more credibility at rapping than anybody in Korea because of their proximity to the genre's source.

As *Show Me the Money* gained notoriety, I was constantly asked by fans and friends alike if I would ever try out for the show. An Mnet producer even hit me up directly to ask me to audition. I always said no, and it wasn't a particularly difficult decision. First of all, it would be hard for me to compete in Korean. Even though there had been competitors who survived for a respectable length of time on a mix of perfect English and broken Korean, I didn't feel my language skills were strong enough to compete at the highest level. But more than that, my dreams of being a renowned entertainer are American dreams—I've never dreamed of Korean fame. All of my heroes are American stars. The only reason I even considered it was the thought of gaining Korean clout that might finally impress my dad. It was the only way I knew to get on his radar.

If I'm being honest, I felt a little bit of envy—and a tiny bit of hate—toward KA rappers who moved to Korea to further their careers. I'd ask myself, *Why would I perform in a whole different language just to blow up?* It didn't seem authentic, like they were mastering Korean not because they were passionate about the language or Korean hip-hop, but because it offered a quicker path toward money and fame.

Is it harder to be a Korean American rapper in America or in Korea? It's a good question. There are two sides to it. I stuck around in a country where there's less of a chance for someone who looks like me to blow up in entertainment. Meanwhile, those who move to Korea are trying to make it in a country where there might be a better chance to make a living—but no matter how big they get, they will forever be viewed as outsider. Neither route is easy, and I can't fault anyone for trying to find a solution to make their career work. Still, I always felt like we should've kept our best representatives in America. When those gyopos were pursuing their rap dreams in Korea, we could've had the illest KA rappers pushing the culture forward here. Instead, they built their community in Asia and to some degree used the currency of their Americanness to buy their way in. Maybe this speaks to my own personal frustration of feeling like I had to battle and represent on behalf of Koreans—and Asians—alone in the States, when everyone who could've been a worthy ally seemed to abandon me and jump ship.

I also had a fear of leaning *too* far into my Korean side, which I thought would mean losing all the work that I'd put into my Americanness. I had toiled so hard to stake a claim in American entertainment, inching forward every year; I didn't want to lose my place. It's like I imagined that one day someone was gonna hand-deliver me a card that read, "You're the next Asian to blow up in America!" and if I moved to Korea, I would never get it. Of course, that was a silly thought because the Internet flattened everything, and Korea was well on its way to becoming a global powerhouse in entertainment. It wasn't a zero-sum game. Not only could you live anywhere and become an international star, but it was almost doubly so if you made it big in Korea.

It all goes back to the gyopo conundrum I mentioned earlier, that indoctrinated belief we have of not fitting in anywhere. Here's the thing: Whether I was standing out as a Chino amongst my Latino friends, or as an Asian MC in South Central, I *liked* not fitting in. I thrived on being the oddball, the weird one, the lone Asian face in the crew picture. The gyopos who embraced their authentic uniqueness helped boost the rise of subcultures in Seoul—and that extended into the K-pop world, with my friends and collaborators like Jay Park and Jessi.

Speaking of K-pop—and at the risk of pissing off any K-pop stans who are reading this—I can't say I'm a huge fan of the genre. But I do get why it's so popular. K-pop is the absolute epitome of pop, so much so that you can use it as a verb: It fucking *pops*—it's colorful, it's energetic, and K-pop idols basically look like synchronized anime characters. (*KPop Demon Hunters* is the ultimate manifestation of that.) It's hard not to be fascinated by it. However, I look at it more as a business model, a system, a formula; it doesn't start with the artists; it starts with the corporations.

I've been to plenty of K-pop shows, and the manufactured feel of the performers leaves me cold. Good performance is about communicating with the crowd on a personal level. Instead, K-pop artists create an optical illusion to follow: five (or so) well-dressed entertainers with similar symmetry and proportions, moving together, perfectly in sync. I can't deny that being an idol requires tremendous discipline and sacrifice. (I got so good at freestyling precisely because it requires so little repetition.) Trainees must take classes, practice, and adhere to a set schedule with little personal freedom. As an artist, the advantage of that is you don't have to figure out your career alone—there's a team figuring it out for you. So maybe I have some resentment toward K-pop artists too. My whole career was DIY—do you know how exhausting that shit is? Like, lugging half of your own closet to a photo shoot and putting together all the looks by yourself? Or mixing and mastering your own songs right after you dropped the vocals in the booth? I guess I'm just envious too. A K-pop group can have only ten songs in their entire catalog and headline Coachella.

My views on K-pop are not only shaped by my own struggles as an indie artist but also my upbringing as an American. I respect K-pop idols as people trying to make a living, but not as artists, because they often lack the freedom to fully express themselves. Whenever I reach out to a K-pop artist or somebody affiliated with a K-pop label, there are so many stakeholders who have to weigh in that it feels like no individual in K-pop can make a decision for themselves. Either they're not allowed to make personal choices, or they're not pushing for that autonomy for fear of being exiled from the system. And that's why Jay Park's such a G.

My K-Pop Homie

I first met Jay Park in L.A. shortly after he got kicked out of Korea in late 2009 and forced to move back with his parents near Seattle. He started his own YouTube channel and subscribed to three accounts—@dumbfoundead happened to be one of them. I hadn't even noticed. Then, out of nowhere, Jay's fans started hitting me up in the comments. "Yo, this huge K-pop star is following you." I had no idea who he was. I did a quick YouTube search of his name, and a local Seattle news video popped up: "One of the most popular pop stars in South Korea," the reporter said, "is holed up in—of all places—his parents' modest home in Edmonds." The next video I clicked, from a few months before, showed legions of girls holding up signs and wailing as Jay solemnly walked toward departures at Incheon Airport. I asked my mom, "Do you know who Jay Park is?" She knew immediately, which meant he had to be a pretty big deal.

What I didn't know then but know now is this: Jay grew up a hip-hop-loving B-boy outside of Seattle who, while still in high school, entered a local audition for visiting scouts from mega K-pop label JYP Entertainment. He was selected and plucked out of the States and moved to Korea in 2005 at age seventeen—having never lived there and not speaking the language—to become a K-pop trainee. Three years later, having survived an intensive curriculum of idol training, Jay emerged as the leader of a seven-member boy group called 2PM. The group debuted in 2008 to rousing success, and Jay was on the verge of stardom as a K-pop idol. Then, on the eve of the release of 2PM's first album, it all came crashing down. A Korean netizen unearthed old posts from Jay's private MySpace page from 2005, when he had barely assimilated to Korea as a trainee. In those damning posts, Jay wrote to a friend, "Korea is g—y" and "I hate Koreans." The public backlash was swift and merciless; Jay was essentially forced out of 2PM and returned to the US in September 2009 as an exiled K-pop idol. And that's when—living at his childhood home, working at a tire shop, and uploading song covers to YouTube—Jay Park first appeared on my radar.

I sent him a simple message—"Yo, whenever you're in L.A., let's link up"—and that's all it took. When I first saw him, I thought, *Who the fuck is this pretty boy?* He showed up to my shitty MacArthur Park studio apartment dressed down but still looking every bit the K-pop star: super light skin, delicate features, shaved lines in his hair, and not a single tattoo. No Ktown fools looked as clean as this guy. I had since learned a bit about his situation, so I expected Jay to seem down and out, but his vibe was positive—and, as I learned both then and later, extremely collaborative. We recorded the song "Clouds"—Jay's first new music since 2PM—in my roach-infested closet booth, with a singer named Clara on the hook. We filmed the session as a music video and uploaded it right away. It felt casual at the time, but looking back, that song feels especially meaningful given where Jay is today.

Fifteen years later, Jay and I remain good friends. Here's the story of his comeback in one sentence: He returned to Korea the summer after we made "Clouds," restarted his music career as a solo artist, released a string of hugely successful albums, was wholeheartedly accepted back into the Korean entertainment world, founded two indie record labels, and is now a legit global superstar—and doing it all on his own terms. (Jay and I even performed together in Seoul at the R-16 afterparty in 2013.) I met Jay at a time when he was the ultimate underdog, and that immediately resonated with me, because I always considered myself one. (Is there such a thing as an Asian American *over*dog in entertainment?) Some juvenile mistakes thrust Jay to the bottom, and he grinded his way back to the top. That inspired me.

I'm proud to have played even a tiny role in Jay's journey back. "Clouds" came at his career low point, and later, I introduced him to the Korean rapper Dok2, whom I met on tour with Epik High. Dok2, of Filipino and Korean descent, was the most swagged-out underground Korean rapper and eager to expand into the K-pop world. Jay, conversely, was a K-pop figure who wanted more hip-hop credibility. The two hit it off instantly, forming a creative partnership that fueled Jay's resurgence.

This goes back to why I respect Jay so much for bucking the system. When he emerged on the Korean scene, he was a child of hip-hop. And even post-2PM, when he regained his status as a K-pop star, he was the only K-pop dude who continued to pursue hip-hop shit, even working with artists far from his level. He lent his personal brand to boost their profiles. Hip-hop has always been in his veins.

Of course, there are other K-pop artists who have charted their own path upon achieving breakout success, like G-Dragon or RM of BTS. But it was only after many years of following the rules that they had the freedom to break them. Gyopos like Jay and Jessi pushed K-pop's boundaries and infused it with American-style individuality, even in the face of severe backlash. Before them there was Drunken Tiger or Teddy of 1TYM, who went to high school near L.A. and went on to mastermind the groups 2NE1 and BLACKPINK for YG Entertainment. Teddy hired my good friend Danny Chung from Philly to his imprint, The Black Label. Danny has since cowritten a handful of top ten hits for BLACKPINK as well as chart-toppers off the *KPop Demon Hunters* soundtrack.

It's no wonder why every new K-pop group has at least one gyopo on the team—either as a member or behind the scenes—to slip in a little more swag and edge to a genre that sorely needs it. When K-pop hit a brief lull in 2024, triggered by BTS's military hiatus and NewJeans's legal meltdown, the genre regained the global spotlight on the strength of *KPop Demon Hunters* and HYBE's girl group KATSEYE—the former powered by gyopos, and the latter the first successful K-pop group with a majority non-Korean lineup. K-pop's next wave might very well rest on the backs of gyopo talent—with the caveat that one misstep by any of them in the public eye could be a career ender. They're not all built like Jay.

Rhyme-Lingual

In 2012, I appeared on national TV for the first time, on Carson Daly's late-night show *Last Call*. It was a pretaped segment, filmed on location in Ktown. In the intro, Carson described me as "a Korean American rapper named Dumbfoundead." Of course. Up until then, I'd always bristled at the need for an ethnic designation—as if "Korean American rapper" were part of my name. That's how the press always referred to me, and whether I liked it or not, that's what people saw. I thought, *I'm a rapper first*, and it felt more badass to *not* have my racial identity follow me around. But over time, I realized it was pointless to try to run away from my ethnicity—and ultimately, counterproductive. There was power in owning it. I learned that lesson from Black artists and entertainers, who command respect by leaning into who they are.

My visits to Korea helped me understand what I represented. I started embracing the label: Korean American rapper. Rap had taken me to Project Blowed, where Black art and Black power were at the forefront in a historically Afrocentric neighborhood. Rap also took me to Korea, the motherland, where I saw that Korean American representation could have a global impact. In turn, I felt not only a duty to represent, but also saw the opportunity to be a pioneer. Of course, I wasn't the first. For example, there was Margaret Cho, who took a lot of heat from the Korean community in the nineties for being outspoken about drugs and LGBTQ issues. Bobby Lee, in his own way, showed an unfiltered side of Asian America. It's easier for Asian entertainers today because of groundbreakers like them.

I kept finding excuses to go back to Korea. The more artists I met and friends I made, the easier it became to justify the trips.

The longest I stayed in Korea was for three months in 2016. I had signed a deal to record a trio of albums there, collaborating with Korean artists. But it was about more than the music—I got to play out my fantasy of living in the motherland. One of those albums was the five-song EP *Foreigner*. I recorded the entire project in Seoul and worked with Korea-based artists like Dok2, Simon Dominic, Jessi, and GSoul. Though I rapped mostly in English, the two biggest songs—"Hyung" and "Mul"—were recorded using a strategic hack to sidestep my lack of Korean fluency. I took one Korean word and turned it into a repeated hook.

Being based in Korea, even for a short time, I started to figure out how the country became a leader in music and pop culture. In America, everyone is quick to break the rules. In the early years of my career, all I wanted to do was go against the grain, without even fully understanding what I was rebelling against. We idolize the lifestyle and the freedom more than the craft in the States. In Korea, they learn the rules first, then break them after. It requires discipline and boundaries. And, ironically, the more boundaries you have, the more creative you get, because it forces you to find clever loopholes to circumvent them. It reminds me of how Ben Caldwell wouldn't let MCs use curse words at Project Blowed; that took away a crutch from rappers who relied on them as filler and made them think of other ways to express themselves.

I didn't grow up thinking Korean culture was cool—maybe that was internalized hate, but it was also because I didn't know better. I always thought my American side was cooler than my Korean side. Actually, come to think of it, I thought of *myself* as cool, as an individual, which had nothing to do with me being Korean *or* American. My attitude changed, as it did for many Korean Americans, as I visited Korea more often. Clubs like Itaewon's Cakeshop, which opened in 2012, felt more progressive and cutting-edge than anything back in L.A. When Korean culture started becoming more prominent globally, I realized that maybe I'd even contributed to the coolness of being Korean. However, I never ended up fully committing to life in Korea beyond that three-month stint in 2016. Being a part-time visitor or a tourist was one thing, but the thought of dealing with day-to-day life in Seoul—the hyunging, the language barrier, the relative lack of diversity—made permanent relocation less appealing. Still, it remains my favorite place to visit in the world.

The funny thing is, despite never being a K-pop fan, I undeniably benefitted from the Korean wave. I cohosted a season of a K-pop talk show on Mnet America with Danny from 1TYM; I freestyled live on stage with RM and interviewed BTS (among other K-pop groups) before they blew up; and I've made countless friends in the K-pop world, many of whom I still see whenever I'm in Seoul. I've paid my K-pop dues, and it's come back around. As my underground hip-hop fans thinned out in the 2010s, their numbers were replenished by K-pop enthusiasts. My crowds transformed from backpack-toting blunt smokers to kids waving glow sticks and LED signs. This unexpected influx has extended my longevity in the game. Ironically, it has also brought me full circle to the identity I'd once resisted. After all, I am a Korean American rapper.

CHAPTER ELEVEN

PLAYING DUMB

I've put out hundreds of songs over the years and recorded even more than that, but these are the eight that stick out most in my mind. Some are among my biggest hits, while others are more obscure and just mean something special to me. To my fans, who have tatted some of these lyrics on their bodies—here's hoping that both the ink and the songs have held up. This list isn't ranked in order of release or from best to worst. Consider it more like a playlist that has a mix of the sentimental and the silly, covering different milestones in my career. Each one tells its own story.

"Are We There Yet," 2011

Everyone loves a good mama song. Kanye has "Hey Mama." 2Pac has "Dear Mama." Eminem has "Cleanin' Out My Closet." I've felt all of those emotions at different times: Ye's pride, Pac's gratitude, and even Em's resentment. My own version was "Are We There Yet." The first verse is a tribute to my mother's journey across the border with me and my sister. LoDef's beat already felt nostalgic—it sounded like it was holding back tears. The hook fit so perfectly that I could just let the instrumental breathe.

Each verse builds toward that restless question. In the first verse, I'm directing it to my mom; then I'm talking to a girl about a situationship; and finally, I'm checking in on myself. *'Cause when things are going well, I get gassed up / That's when I look into the mirror and I ask / Tell me, brother, are we there yet?* It was a reminder to myself to not get too comfortable, even as my career took off. Fifteen years later, my perspective is a little different. I recently read an Earl Sweatshirt quote that resonated with me: "I feel like the goal of my life has been to stay alive long enough for all of the clichés to become profound." It's true—the journey really is the destination.

"Jam Session 2.0," 2010

The most watched video on my YouTube channel isn't even a song. It's a twenty-nine-second clip titled "Dumbfoundead Freestyle Battle Knock Out." It's amateur footage of a battle that suddenly turns physical when my opponent shoves me. I respond with a Jackie Chan roundhouse that drops him flat. The cypher goes bananas as the camera shakily captures the chaos. To this day, people still ask, "Was the kick real?" Which proves you don't need AI to fool the masses. Here's the truth: It was a choreographed stunt, with world-class martial artist Travis Wong playing my stunt double. Five minutes of shooting, over five million views. This viral marketing move launched the post-battle phase of my career.

The stunt was the brainchild of my manager, Brian Lee. When I met him, my chest was puffed out because I had battles on YouTube with millions of views. Brian wasn't impressed. "Those videos are on other people's channels, not your own," he said. "You're not monetizing." I didn't even know what "monetize" meant, much less how to do it. So, we cooked up the kung-fu kick video, leaning into my Asian battle-rapper identity. It was only my third YouTube upload, and it pulled 50,000 new subscribers overnight. The following year, I went ham on the platform—thirty-six videos in 2010, a new one almost every week. Instead of spending a month prepping for a single battle that would live on someone else's channel, I was creating content for myself—and *monetizing* it.

After the kick video hit, Brian kept pushing me to think bigger. "Jam Session 2.0" was another of his brainstorms. The description says it all: "eight people, with five instruments, originally from four continents, speaking three languages, for one song." Social media made online collaboration the new wave, and we gave it a musical twist—a global jam session with three artists backed by a DJ, piano, guitar, and drum machine. Even CNN covered it. My verses emphasized the interconnectivity.

It started with a verse, each person just came and joined in
Some are complete strangers, some only teenagers
All of us creators
We are the dreammakers
Internationally transmittin' through bandwidth
Passin' this band's passion so the masses can jam with you

The Internet tore down the gatekeepers that historically kept label-less rappers like me on the fringes. We didn't need a *Rolling Stone* feature to get noticed—we carved out our own space. Every piece of content we put out was produced by us, in-house. This was the experimental era of YouTube, and I was in the lab cookin'.

"Cell Phone" f/ Breezy Lovejoy & Wax, 2012

There was a minute when Breezy (now known as Anderson .Paak), Wax, and I were plotting a trio called A Pyramid Scheme. Album, merch, tour . . . *aaaaaaand* then Anderson got too famous, so we scrapped the whole thing. Could've been a cute United Colors of Benetton rap group. Alas. At least we left behind "Cell Phone." It's a goofy little ditty pulled straight from our own lives: waking up with a crushing hangover and realizing your phone has gone missing.

Wax and I had already dropped an entire collab album, *Clockwise*, the year before. I first found him through the 2010s YouTube rap wave—back when names like DeStorm, Traphik (aka Timothy DeLaGhetto), and Prince Ea made their names on the platform. Most of those YouTube rappers were cool, but Wax was the only one who made me go *whoa*. A Baltimore dude who could spit *and* play mad instruments, Wax was the real deal. We clicked instantly.

"Cell Phone" was a single off my first official album, *DFD*. Wax and Anderson were two of my favorite collaborators. In fact, Anderson went on to produce my entire next album, *Take the Stares*. What makes this song special is that it captures a moment when the three of us were running through the L.A. indie music scene, not taking ourselves too seriously. We even went on a little cross-country tour together called "Wintervention" at the end of 2013. What a time to be alive.

"It G Ma (Remix)," Keith Ape f/ Waka Flocka Flame, Dumbfoundead, Father & A$AP Ferg, 2015

New Year's Day 2015 dropped a bomb on Korean hip-hop. That was when the original "It G Ma" premiered on YouTube—out of nowhere, from an artist named Keith Ape. The video featured a squad of Korean and Japanese homies, including KOHH (now Yuki Chiba), wilding out in ways that people hadn't seen before from Asian rappers. The internet had flattened the world so much that musical influences could spread in real time—"It G Ma" was clearly inspired by OG Maco's "U Guessed It"—but Keith and his crew twisted it into something new. "It G Ma" means "don't forget" in Korean, and you couldn't.

The song grabbed me before it went viral. At the time, I was managed by Sean Miyashiro, who had just launched 88Rising, a company in search of cool Asian artists. I showed Sean the video, we hopped on a FaceTime with Keith, and shit just started moving like, "Let's sign you. Let's do an American remix. Let's fly you out for South by Southwest." The iron was hot, and we swung that motherfucker *hard*. Keith was the first artist I helped turn into a legit business venture. (The following year, I put Sean on to a sixteen-year-old from Indonesia who looked like a mathlete but rapped like a trap star—you know him now as Rich Brian.) With 88Rising newly on the scene and scores of talented young musicians emerging across Asia, it was an exciting time to be an Asian artist. I made sure to lock in my spot on the "It G Ma" remix. Sean stacked the roster with 2015 all-stars: Waka Flocka Flame, Father, and A$AP Ferg. We shot the music video with Complex in Bushwick and Flushing, New York. A couple more artists recorded verses but didn't make the cut. Yung Gleesh and Yung Lean were both supposed to be on the remix, but Gleesh caught a charge, and Lean's manager passed away. People still bring up my verse to me—it aged well. *Not me, motherfuckers, top three, I cannot be explained / Got the homie Keith Ape with a briefcase and a .38 / Looking for the nearest currency exchange.* Truth is, I still prefer the original—it didn't even need a remix. But its mere existence pointed to a growing East–West movement in music.

That spring and summer, we mobbed with Keith and his Cohort crew across the US: SXSW in Texas, SOB's in NYC, and Spam N Eggs in L.A. They got to experience the American rap life up close—the good, the bad, the mosh pits, the drugs. It was the era of sipping lean and popping pills. Keith got a little caught up in that stuff, and it slowed his momentum. But even if the movement was short-lived, the moment was legendary. To this day, if you play those first few notes of "It G Ma" at any Asian function, people go crazy. It's the "Gangnam Style" of Korean rap, and I was happy to be a small part of it. Underwater squad! Skrrt skrrt skrrt!

"Safe," 2016

I was watching the Oscars when my face suddenly got hot. Host Chris Rock had trotted out a trio of Asian kids and introduced them as the accountants at PricewaterhouseCoopers. "If anybody is upset about that joke," he added, "just tweet about it on your phone—which was also made by these kids." An hour later, Sacha Baron Cohen, in full Ali G, cracked about "little yellow people with tiny dongs." His punchline pointed to the Minions, but we all knew who he meant. My blood boiled. The irony is, that year's ceremony was shrouded in the #OscarsSoWhite controversy. Not only did that convo apparently leave out Asians, but we also caught random strays. I redirected my anger into a song.

The other night I watched the Oscars
And the roster of the only yellow men were all statues
We a quarter of the population
There's a room of fuckin' 1-percenters laughing at you

I called it "Safe," because that's how people see Asians—like nothing will happen if you insult us. The hook says it plainly: *You took me as safe / That was your first mistake / Who said I was safe?* My hyung DPD pitched the video concept—superimposing my face into scenes from classic films and TV shows, from *The Shining* and *Pulp Fiction* to *Game of Thrones* and *Friends.* If Hollywood wasn't going to invite me in, I'd put myself there. We uploaded the video to YouTube less than three months after the Oscars. It somehow dodged a copyright strike and went viral. To this day, it's my most viewed music video.

At the conclusion of the "Safe" clip, I'm replaced by a white version of myself—even in this fantasy, whitewashing prevails. But in the decade since, Asian faces—including my own—are on screen in ways Chris Rock and Ali G couldn't fathom back then. We're not so safe anymore.

"형 (Hyung)" f/ Tiger JK, Simon Dominic & Dok2, 2017

There's good and bad to "hyung shit"—the etiquette around older male figures in Korean culture. A close hyung is supposed to guide and protect you, taking you under his wing. The basic rules are simple—if he's older, you bow upon greeting, use polite Korean verb endings, pour and receive drinks with two hands, and turn your face when you sip. And hyungs always pick up the check.

The downside, though, is that dongsaengs are obligated to show deference even if their hyungs haven't earned it. At best, it's like Confucius-backed peer pressure; at worst, it's like being a frat pledge for life. "Hyung," the most popular of my Korean songs, addresses that dichotomy. On the first half of the hook, I declare, *I'm on my hyung shit*—an elder demanding respect. Then I flip it: *But fuck all that hyung shit!* Because in the end, age ain't nothing but a number.

Funnily enough, it took a rapper who grew up in Korea to inspire that rebuttal. The original hook had only the first part. But when I heard Dok2's verse, he rapped, *Fuck all that hyung-hyung-hyung shit.* It sounded so hard. As a gyopo, I'd been trying to honor Korean culture, but the truth is, I never believed in blind obedience based on birth year. When I heard Dok2 say he's not down with it, either, I switched up the hook to add the *fuck all that hyung shit* line. It became much doper after that.

Dok2 and Simon Dominic are some of my closest Korean rapper homies. Simon has the pretty face of an idol and the deep voice of an anime villain. In his verse, he sneak-dissed me—he says (in Korean) that even though he's two years older, my face is more hyung than his. Basically, I might be a Ktown OG, but I look like an old head. It's classic rap tradition to sneak in a jab at someone on the same track, so I didn't get too offended. Besides, Simon's always been a great hyung to me when I visit Korea. Adding JK—the super hyung of Korean rap—to the outro was the final stamp of approval.

"Hyung" is one of my favorite songs to perform because it always gets the crowd hype. Jimmy O. Yang even used it as his walk-on music for a stand-up special. As his hyung, I approve. But fuck all that hyung shit.

"Love Is a Song (DFD Remix)," 2011

What's wrong with writing another love song?
'Cause all you got is love songs when the love's gone

I'm a romantic. Been like that ever since I made mixtapes for crushes in fourth grade. Since then, I've handwritten letters, commissioned illustrations, and even supported the DJ careers of women who couldn't mix for shit. I tend to view relationships through rom com–tinted glasses—*The Wedding Singer*, even the doomed love of *Romeo + Juliet*. Probably because I never had a healthy model of love growing up, I clung to movie fantasies. I've never been great at saying how I feel, though—which is why love songs are so clutch.

"Love Is a Song" started as an instrumental from my hyung DJ Soulscape's 2003 *Lovers* album. With his blessing, I took the beat and wrote from the perspective of a player desperate to make amends. *You say I'm so sweet, but only on beats / 'Cause in person I always seem to say the wrong thing.* We shot the video at Beer Belly, a popular Ktown bar, where I pleaded my case with one girl before pivoting straight to the next. Pretty much the story of my life in under three minutes.

I've written plenty more love songs since, each for different reasons. "No More Sunny Days" was about an immigrant bartender—guess her name—whom I dated for three months and who ghosted me when I said I wasn't ready to commit.

We had language barriers but we broke it down
She ain't understand, but laughed when we joked around
She said let's take it further, I said let's slow it down
Only now do I realize that it's over

Usually, I'm more subliminal, like in my COVID-era track "Outside." That one was about a crush on my friend Steffie. *'Til then Imma stay put, lightin' up my eighth wood / Loadin' up on baked goods*—@baikedguds was her IG handle—*hard to love a Virgo, whippin' in her turbo*—referring to her sign and the Porsche she drove. I sent it to her, and she loved it. Musicians have a cheat code, what can I say?

Whenever I write a song aimed at someone specific—whether we've broken up or haven't even dated yet—I always want that girl to hear it. Some artists write love songs because they're cathartic; I write them because I can't always say things directly. A muse brings out some of my most focused writing because I'm trying to impress them. I wish I'd written a song for my last partner before we broke up. She deserves her own soundtrack.

"Washed," 2018

Some years ago, at an 88Rising party, an Asian dude in his early twenties came up to me. He pulled out his phone and showed me a picture of a scrawny teen posing awkwardly next to me. "That's us, man!" he said. That kid grew up to be Keshi, who just sold out Madison Square Garden. More recently, I blindly DMed the singer Ejae, of the No. 1 song "Golden" and *KPop Demon Hunters* fame. She hit me back with "Uhhh . . . legend." Moments like that feel great—inspiring younger artists and getting my flowers. I was once the prodigy learning the ropes from the OGs. Now I'm the OG.

Then there are humbling moments. Like when a fan comes up and says, "I used to listen to you when I was in middle school," as if I were Kurtis Blow or something. Or the time I was cruising down the street on a Bird scooter, and a Bentley pulled up next to me. A white dude lowered the driver's-side window, yelling, "Dumb, I'm a huge fan!" Then he peeled off in his $300,000 car, and I looked down at my scooter feeling . . . washed.

Once I passed thirty, I started to feel it, even if I have Peter Pan Syndrome. Rap has historically been a young man's sport. I went from yelling "Fuck the police" to paying my parking tickets on time. Meanwhile, I watched friends like Awkwafina and Anderson blow up as I wondered, *Where am I going with my life?* That question birthed "Washed."

I put them on the wave
But today I'm feelin' washed
And off my game
And I feel my age

The tone was lighthearted and self-deprecating, and the video doubled down: I cast my hyung Jongman Kim to play an older, hapless version of me. Future Dumb is an alcoholic living out of a dingy hotel room, bitter that the world has passed him by. It's funny because it's sad.

And yet, the lyrics are still defiant.

A&R'ed the hardest artists
But you'd never know, 'cause I'm modest
True, I never signed on that dotted
But came out the game cum laude

At forty, I'm realizing that the chip on my shoulder weighs me down. Gratitude feels lighter, appreciating what I did instead of regretting what I didn't. The validation I care about is from loved ones and peers I respect. And anyway, rappers today are thriving past forty and even into their fifties. A couple of years ago, I even wrote a pilot for Peacock about a washed-up thirtysomething rapper, loosely based on my life. Now it feels outdated.

Did what I came to do, Hollis sings on the outro. *Got nothing left to prove.* I'm still here. And I'm good with that.

CHAPTER TWELVE

BIG DUMMIE

The Poster Syndrome

The Internet is a global stage with no promoters, no velvet ropes, no friction. I jumped on it every chance I got. It wasn't so different from when I'd jump in front of the TV so my father couldn't ignore me—if I didn't force myself into the frame, I'd disappear entirely. Online, the instant feedback loop gave me the love and validation I desperately longed for to feel good about myself. Compliments from strangers were saved for posterity. But so too were the insults. I'd absorb the negativity to justify the narrative that I wasn't good enough. One hateful comment could ruin my night, sometimes my week. Although I was used to getting shit on—by my dad, local haters, or a hostile battle crowd—those moments were fleeting. I could brush them off and walk away. Negative online comments were different. Brutally honest and highly specific, they cut deeper and lingered longer.

My manager Brian tried to turn that sting into motivational fuel. In the spring of 2011, he surprised me with a strange gift: a laminated poster of hate comments I'd received on YouTube. Brian cherry-picked the ones he knew would hit a nerve:

> *Dude is about as overrated as it gets. I understand he's funny, but there are a lot of funny people. A lot more naturally funny people with better jokes that are better written.*
>
> *It's clearly just a case of "right place, right time" kind of thing. He was basically able to capitalize off of a gimmick (Asian vs. Asian).*
>
> *Dumbfoundead is a good battler, just like Yao Ming is a good basketball player; but there's nothing really exceptional about them besides the fact they're ASIAN!!!!*

The poster poked at insecurities I already had about my merits as a commercially viable rapper and whether or not I could break out of the kimchi circuit. Across the top, Brian had printed: "They want you to fail and the only way to win is if the talent is undeniable." Across the bottom: "No substitute for hard work."

"Hang it where you'll see it every day," he told me. As tough as it was to read, I understood what he was trying to do. He was like a coach giving his star player the "Nobody believes in you" speech in laminated form.

The truth was, in my midtwenties, I was coasting. Everyone in my circle constantly told me I was the shit. Ktown loved me. The battle-rap world respected me. Asian America looked up to me. Women wanted to know me. What more did I need? But Brian kept pushing me to see the bigger picture—and honestly, he was right. I preferred partying to productivity. Fear and a lack of work ethic held me back. I knew I wanted more, but I wasn't ready to sacrifice for it. Looking back now, it's clear I had deeper issues. I was a functioning alcoholic and drug addict, though I didn't admit it then. Hindsight makes it obvious. Brian tried to pull me out of that cycle with books, films, and ideas that expanded my perspective—and yeah, a laminated poster full of YouTube hate.

I'd always admired greatness and wanted to reach it for myself. But once you hit the first level of success, it's tempting to stop climbing. You think, *I made it this far, maybe I should just enjoy this.* Reaching the next level is way harder. As they say, getting good is easy; becoming great is the real challenge—which is why there are so few true greats. When I first saw Anderson .Paak, I knew he'd be one of them.

Breezy & the Boot Camp

I met Anderson around 2010, back when he was still Breezy Lovejoy. Yes, Breezy Lovejoy. He already had a little buzz in the underground L.A. scene. This was the post-Blowed era, when new showcases were popping up for the next wave of talent. Two of my old Swim Team homies from Blowed put me on. VerBS was throwing Bananas, a regular event at KAOS in Leimert Park. It carried the Blowed spirit, only with more eclectic energy: Black kids mixing indie rock, left-field R&B, and all kinds of genre-bending experiments. Anderson had torn it down there, and VerBS told me to keep an eye out. My boy Lyraflip was running a similar monthly called the Melting Pot.

When I saw "Breezy Lovejoy" on the flyer, I pulled up. And there he was: singing, rapping, and playing the drums at the same damn time. The texture of his voice grabbed my ear; it was gravelly and buttery all at once, a bluesman's grit with a SoCal cool. Backed by his band, Free Nationals, Anderson slid from gospel to R&B to trap with an ease that felt unreal. Sweating and smiling under the lights, he was killing it effortlessly, with swag. I was blown away.

After the show, I made a beeline for the green room. There, I met Anderson's wife, who was pregnant with their son Soul. She was a Korean FOB, so she was familiar with my name.

When I introduced myself to Anderson, I cut straight to it. "That was dope, man. I definitely want to get you in the studio. Want to work on stuff together?"

He flashed his million-watt smile. "Let's do it," he said.

I learned quickly that we shared a lot in common. We are both Aquariuses, born weeks apart in 1986. He grew up in Oxnard, about sixty miles west of L.A., raised primarily by his Black-Korean mother. (His estranged dad was Black.) Through his wife, Anderson was pretty tapped into Korean culture. He'd been playing drums in his family church since he was a kid and earned the "Breezy" nickname because he farted so much. He later added "Lovejoy" because he thought it sounded smooth. From the jump, Anderson was easy to work with. His natural charisma was magnetic, and his energy was contagious. What struck me most was his joyful spirit. Coming from the world of battle rap, I was surrounded by negativity and burnouts. Anderson was like a ray of light, and I needed it.

And Jesus . . . the talent. I'd been around some gifted artists before, but Anderson was something different. Music poured out of him so freely that it was impossible not to feel it. His talent was so incredible that it gave me imposter syndrome—I actually felt guilty having a bigger fan base than he did. It was discouraging, yet inspiring. Humbling. There are artists you encounter who you know will become competition; true greatness, however, you want on your side.

When we first linked, I was deep into recording my first official solo album. Within a month, he was on nearly half of the tracks—whether behind the boards or on the chorus—adding a musicality that improved the sound. That album, *DFD*, came out at the end of 2011. The following year, Anderson executive-produced the follow-up, *Take the Stares*. His artistry pushed me to raise my game.

I started taking him on tour, and that's when I began to understand that his approach stretched beyond what I was used to. As a freestyler, I'd go into shows thinking only about the words I'd be spitting that night. Anderson considered the entire package. In the spring of 2013, we did a few sold-out shows in London—randomly, the Nepalese community there loved me—and Anderson came out to open for me wearing a full jumpsuit. When I hit the stage, I cracked a quick joke—"Make some noise for Breezy Lovejoy—he's out here looking like a janitor!"—and moved on. Afterward, he pulled me aside, dead serious. "Yo fam, don't say shit like that. This is all part of the vision." It was the angriest I'd ever seen him. I realized a true showman brands their look; for Anderson, every detail mattered. I never publicly roasted his fits like that again—and believe me, he's worn some doozies since.

During that era, we were inseparable. Everyone I introduced him to saw the same thing I did: a generational talent. And we all wanted him to win. He hustled nonstop—playing gigs with other crews, pitching himself to labels, and drumming at church every Sunday. If he hadn't broken through yet, it wasn't for lack of trying. Turns out his gift was also his curse: He could play so many genres that nobody knew how to market him. The industry liked their artists in neat boxes, and Anderson was a wild card.

I knew what my manager Brian had done for me, helping me strategize and stay focused, so I connected the dots. "You *have* to work with this guy," I told Brian. At the time, Anderson had even less momentum than I did, and it's wild to think about now—that I had to convince someone to manage Anderson .Paak. But Brian agreed.

As talented as he was, Anderson wasn't the most disciplined cat. Brian was already struggling to keep me on task, so he took matters into his own hands. His friend's family owned an apartment building in Culver City, and Brian rented a two-bedroom there. He set up another two-bedroom for me on a different floor. In his spare room, he built a studio for Anderson, since he didn't have one at the time. (He didn't even have a car.) For a few summers straight, Brian stayed on our asses and pushed us to work. He checked our drinking and partying, and for the first time in my life, I complied. My parents had never been strict, so I wasn't used to that kind of discipline. I'd always bullshitted my way past them, teachers, and authority figures. But I couldn't smooth-talk Brian. He'd checkmate me every time. Eventually, I put my head down and grinded. Anderson went even harder: He'd bike over from Venice to Culver City and let himself into my apartment with a key I gave him. I'd come home from a late night out and find him still there, hunched over the mic. He was pulling all-nighters, churning out songs until neighbors complained. During that stretch, Anderson created most of what became

Venice and a few joints for *Malibu*. I'd wake up to demo versions of records that millions of people would later know by heart. We call that period "Brian's Boot Camp," and it worked.

More than just a drill sergeant, Brian was a marketing madman. He kept two giant whiteboards in his apartment, scribbled with arrows, diagrams, and notes like a college physics lecture. Because Anderson needed a clearer identity, they carefully analyzed the competition. Ironically—prophetically?—one of the albums they broke down was Bruno Mars's 2012 release *Unorthodox Jukebox*, figuring out why it worked. Bruno was a young dude who made old-school soul that appealed to a broad audience—a lane that seemed open for Anderson. They even studied Phil Collins's career, since Anderson was also a frontman who played drums. It's funny now—back then, they were asking themselves how Bruno got his album into Walmart or played at Starbucks. Today, Anderson is one of those artists you hear everywhere. Over time, he carved out that signature Anderson .Paak sound.

Brian's Boot Camp couldn't last forever. We were all ready to move on to different things. I drifted back to Ktown, and Anderson became . . . well, Anderson. In the end, we parted ways with Brian, but we'll always give him credit. He put us on the path.

Wisdumb

We'd both come a long way from Culver City. Anderson became a global star. I was still figuring out what I'd become.

For a time, I was a hero of L.A.'s underground music scene. That was my Hollywood. I'd roll through Ktown spots with Anderson and Awkwafina in tow, and people treated me like a bigshot. I was Vinnie, and they were my Turtles. These days, when I step out with them in the actual Hollywood scene, the roles are reversed. I went from Vinnie to Turtle.

To be clear, Anderson and Awkwafina always show me love—and even take me on expensive trips—for the role I played in their come-ups. They won't let me forget the impact I had on them, and it feels good to know I'm appreciated. Still, it's not easy having two best friends who are some of the most famous people in the world. They don't hang out with most of my other friends—the ones without Wikipedia entries—so I sit in the middle of the gap. It's actually a sweet spot, being just below real fame. I'm big enough to get some of the perks of celebrity—free shit, occasional recognition—but not so big that I've lost personal freedom. (I get dapped up a lot by bouncers and service workers; blue-collar dudes are the backbone of battle rap.) I can say or do pretty much anything I want without sending a PR team into crisis mode. I'm not famous enough for a scandal to derail my whole life. (Knock on wood.) I see firsthand the stress Anderson and Awkwafina deal with constantly. They're always venting to me about being pulled in every direction. It makes me feel grateful for where I'm at right now.

Of course, I want more. Netflix stand-up specials. Big-time movie roles. Fuck it, give me an EGOT. What I really can't stand is when someone says, "Dumb, you have so much potential." Like, motherfucker, I've been in the game for over twenty years! I'm a fucking pioneer! "Potential" isn't a word you want to hear at age forty. Talk to me about payoff.

The moment I achieve something, my mind's already scheming on the next big thing—and getting frustrated if it doesn't happen.

My hyung Bobby Lee sometimes tries to ground me. "What else do you want? You're in movies, you've put out albums, you've toured the world," he'll say. "You're already living the dream." (Note that Bobby is hella rich and famous, so it's easy for him to say.) And he's right. It's wild to think how far I've come from Thursday nights at Leimert Park. When will I feel like I've made it? Or that I'm enough? I don't know.

Even a couple years ago, I felt like I wasn't there yet. Not even close. So, I was relentlessly feeding the content machine, more out of fear than love. The fear of being invisible. Lately, I've learned to chill a little. I've been off social media more than ever, and the quiet gives me peace of mind. It's then that I can better appreciate what I have.

It's all relative. When I go out these days, mad people come up to congratulate me—often for no reason at all. They're like, "Congrats on *everything*," and I realize that to the outside world, it really must look like I'm living the dream.

Filmmaker Salima Koroma, who directed *Bad Rap*, once commented on my Instagram, "I love your life!!"

I told her the truth: "I don't share the depressed moments." What you see is the highlight reel, same as everyone else.

When I reflect on my lows, they often trace to being a lifelong attention junkie. Without the spotlight, I spiral. Which is why I tried to steal my dad's gaze, cracked wise in class, jumped into Blowed cyphers, posted shit online, and chased women. (Or even wrote this book!) Anything to be seen. It's mostly served me well so far. But the older I get, the more I realize that it's a child's need—the love and attention I craved when I was young. I'm forever scared of disappearing. I have friends who don't crave that validation, who work behind the scenes or in low-profile jobs. They seem happy. It makes me rethink what success even is.

So, back to that inescapable question: Are we there yet? The answer is no. Because there is no "there." Only here.

As I rose up the battle ranks, I took on all comers. I applied that mentality to my personal life, turning even relationships into endless competition. Now I follow the age-old adage: Choose your battles. Better to be fueled by love, not hate. The right ones can make you a better rapper, a better man, a better son. My relationship with my father may be a battle I can't win. But I haven't totally given up yet. The petty fights, the "invisible wars"—those I'll gladly concede. The struggle within myself? That one has no winner or loser. It's a lifelong work in progress.

Another memorable rap line: *You only get one shot, do not miss your chance to blow.* Lyrics you'll probably see framed on IKEA posters any day now. Respect to Eminem, but here's the real truth: You get *many* shots in life. You should take the real ones seriously, of course, but if you airball one, another will come around. I know artists who've bricked opportunities, only to thrive later when the timing was right. I may not have that stand-up special yet, but it's a marathon, not a sprint, and I'm the Forrest Gump of this shit. And I'm just getting started.

Fear of failure keeps many people from even trying. But once you take that first step, you'll find others willing to join you. That's true in battles, in music, in anything. Failure isn't as painful as you think. I've failed enough times to know the hurt fades, but the growth stays.

So, here's my final piece of advice: Make as much art as possible before you're dead. You can't win every battle, but you can at least stay in the fight.

ACKNOWLEDGMENTS

I want to thank my mom and dad for the sacrifices they made that allowed me to do what I love. And my sister, Natalie, who has gone through hell and back with me during the roughest times of our youth. My friend and coauthor, Donnie, whom I've spent the last few years becoming brothers with—thank you for your wisdom and honesty and for having my back through this whole process.

Thank you to Charles and Stephanie at Third State for publishing a high-school dropout's book. To Kev, DPD, Virman, Proh, Kirby, and the whole Transparent Agency—you guys are truly the OGs. Thank you for being some of my biggest believers. And thank you to my DJ and brother Zo, who's traveled the world with me and is a pioneer in his own right.

I also want to thank Koreatown, the neighborhood that gave me the confidence to be proud of my culture; and Project Blowed, the open mic that gave me a second family. To my crew, the Swim Team and Thirsty Fish: Open Mike Eagle, AlphaMC, Rogue, VerBS, Lyraflip, Psychosiz, and my brother Sahtyre, who has shared countless battles and shenanigans with me. Nocando—All City Jimmy, James, whatever name you go by now—you'll always be one of my rap heroes.

Anderson .Paak, the brother I never knew I needed—thank you

for your inspiration and guidance as a friend and musician. You're a legend, and we're just getting started. MC Jin, a true trailblazer whom I'm honored to call a friend. Jay Park, a friend for two decades who has accomplished things that are mind-boggling and inspirational. Wax, my partner-in-rhyme and one of the sickest on the mic—thank you for an era of fun. My mentor and friend Brian Lee, who gave me the keys to live the artist life of my dreams.

Thank you to my group chat HYUNG LLC, which has damn near acted as a creative agency, helping filter out the nonsense online and bringing so much joy and laughter throughout my week. Thank you to Rek, Danny, and Rick for your friendship as we were navigating this rap game together as kids. Thank you to Nora, my sister, one of the funniest people alive, for inspiring us all. Steffie, one of my closest friends—it's a blessing to have you in my life; thank you for the free therapy. Dan of Fast Lean Fit, you've changed my life through a healthier mind, body, and spirit. My L.A. big brother Roy Choi, thank you for the love and support. TOKiMONSTA, whom I've admired and come up with in the L.A. scene, thank you for inspiring me. And Brian Yoon, thank you for your beautiful art over the years that essentially branded Dumbfoundead.

Thank you to Seth, Jerold, Fonda, and Andrew at the Bresee Youth Center; Organik; King of the Dot; Grind Time; Lush One; Grady Shon; Intuition; Paul Song; Jaeyoung; Manifest; Café Bleu; Low End Theory; Jeet Kune Flow; Customer Service; Rafa; Andy Hong; Mimi Hong; Kublai Kwon; Tony K; J.U.I.C.E.; Kenny Segal; Abstract Rude; Aceyalone; Badru; Lady Sol; Gaknew; Cre8; Ben Caldwell; Tim Chantarangsu; JustKiddingFilms; Bobby Lee; Eddie Huang; David Choe; Lee Sung Jin; Gene Kam; Gene Hong; Jacqueline Kim; David

Chien; Jose Rios; Free Nationals; Jay Caspian Kang; Ronny Chieng; Jimmy O. Yang; Tiger JK; Alice Han; Lisa Joy; Soonho Choi; Alex Oh; Alex the Intern; Eric and ***Giant Robot***; Michelle Kwon; Turtleboat; Aaron Kai; and the L.A. underground.

Thank you to all the Asian American artists who paved the way, allowing kids like me to talk my shit. Thank you, Hip-Hop!

—Jonnie Park

First and foremost, I want to thank my brother Dumb for trusting me with the opportunity to help tell his story. He's the kind of friend who's always in your ear, hyping you up and pushing you out of your comfort zone. Our friendship continues to inspire me. I forgive him for copying the spelling of my name for his rebrand. Thank you also to his mother, Kitty, and his sister, Nat, for their candor in recalling some difficult times.

Thank you to Charles, Stephanie, and the Third State team for their guidance and patience, and to William LoTurco and NCB for their early advice. Thank you to HYUNG LLC for having my back and keeping me grounded.

Thank you, of course, to my mom and dad, and to my sister, Youna Kwak—brilliant poet and forever inspiration. I love you guys.

And to Korean Americans everywhere who relate to anything in this book: We see you.

—Donnie Kwak

Paint my face on the side of the liquor store when I die
The one on Catalina up on 8th street
Paint me, I wanna be immortalized

—Dumbfoundead, "Murals"

"Dumb Memories"
Artwork by Brian Yoon